TIME
Great Buildings

Clarity: *When British architect Norman Foster renovated Germany's historic parliament building, the Reichstag, he crowned it with a transparent dome*

TIME

MANAGING EDITOR Richard Stengel
ART DIRECTOR D.W. Pine

Great Buildings

ORIGINALLY PUBLISHED IN 2004; REVISED AND UPDATED, 2010

EDITOR Kelly Knauer
DESIGNER Ellen Fanning
PICTURE EDITOR Patricia Cadley
WRITING AND RESEARCH Matthew McCann Fenton; Tresa McBee
COPY EDITOR Bruce Christopher Carr

TIME INC. HOME ENTERTAINMENT

PUBLISHER Richard Fraiman
GENERAL MANAGER Steven Sandonato
EXECUTIVE DIRECTOR, MARKETING SERVICES Carol Pittard
DIRECTOR, RETAIL AND SPECIAL SALES Tom Mifsud
DIRECTOR, NEW PRODUCT DEVELOPMENT Peter Harper
DIRECTOR, BOOKAZINE DEVELOPMENT AND MARKETING Laura Adam
PUBLISHING DIRECTOR, BRAND MARKETING Joy Butts
ASSISTANT GENERAL COUNSEL Helen Wan
BOOK PRODUCTION MANAGER Suzanne Janso
DESIGN AND PREPRESS MANAGER Anne-Michelle Gallero
ASSOCIATE BRAND MANAGER Michela Wilde
ASSOCIATE PREPRESS MANAGER Alex Voznesenskiy

SPECIAL THANKS TO
Christine Austin, Jenny Biloon, Glenn Buonocore, Jim Childs, Susan Chodakiewicz, Rose Cirrincione, Brian Fellows, Jacqueline Fitzgerald, Carrie Frazier, Lauren Hall, Jennifer Jacobs, Brynn Joyce, Mona Li, Robert Marasco, Amy Migliaccio, Kimberly Posa, Brooke Reger, Dave Rozzelle, Ilene Schreider, Adriana Tierno, TIME Imaging, Sydney Webber, Jonathan White

This volume includes text drawn from the work of the following TIME writers: Robert Hughes (Guggenheim Bilbao); Richard Lacayo (Bloch Building, Nelson-Atkins Museum; Burj Khalifa; Cartier Foundation; Cooper Square; Jewish Museum of Berlin); Katherine Tanko (Gherkin Building).

We welcome your comments and suggestions about TIME Books. Please write to us at:
TIME Books, Attention: Book Editors, P.O. Box 11016, Des Moines, IA 50336-1016

To order any of our hardcover Collector's Edition books, please call us at 1-800-327-6388.
Hours: Monday through Friday, 7 a.m.–8 p.m., or Saturday, 7 a.m.–6 p.m., Central Time.

ISBN 10: 1-60320-161-0
ISBN 13: 978-1-60320-161-2
Library of Congress Control Number: 2004104204

To enjoy TIME's frequently updated coverage of current events, visit: **time.com**

Every which way *The designs of Canadian-born U.S. architect Frank Gehry, such as these apartments in Düsseldorf, Germany, forgo conventional straight lines and angles to express Gehry's unique vision*

Contents

Chrysler Building, New York City
Architect William van Alen's spire is a classic of the Art Deco style

Buildings That Astonish

California Academy of Sciences, San Francisco *No, it's not Middle-earth—it's middle California, where the innovative Italian architect Renzo Piano unified a multi-building campus in 2008 by covering the structures with a two-acre "living roof." Porthole windows illuminate the interiors of the buildings.*

The Pyramids

Giza, Egypt • 25th century, B.C.
Architects unknown

Pharaoh Khufu (Cheops, to the Greeks) ruled the land of Kemet, today's Egypt, in the 25th century B.C. The great pyramids he built at Giza are the last survivors of the original Seven Wonders of the World, and they rank among the most massive—and the most mysterious—of mankind's creations. The Great Pyramid, at center, was originally 481 ft. (147 m) high, but time, the elements and human mischief have whittled it down to 449 ft.

Among the pyramids' puzzles: how people who had not invented the wheel and had no sophisticated mechanical devices for hoisting large, heavy objects off the ground were able to haul more than 2 million giant stone blocks (some weighing as much as nine tons) from quarries many miles distant and then raise them hundreds of feet in the air. And how did the ancient Egyptians design a building in which the relationship of the overall height to the length of each side is the same as the ratio of a circle's radius to its circumference, thousands of years before the Greeks discovered pi? The pyramids stand mute, so immovable as to seem immortal. As an Egyptian adage goes, Man fears time, and time fears the pyramids. ∎

The Taj Mahal

Agra, India • 1653
Ahmad Lahouri, chief architect

Mark Twain called it "that soaring bubble of marble." For Rudyard Kipling, it was "the Ivory Gate through which all good dreams come." For the great Indian poet Rabindranath Tagore, it was "a teardrop of love on the cheek of time." But for Shah Jahan, the 17th century Mogul Emperor who built the Taj Mahal ("Crown Palace") in Agra, the building was a tribute to the woman he loved. After the death in 1631 of his favorite wife, Mumtaz Mahal ("Exalted One of the Palace"), with whom he had 14 children in 19 years, the Shah resolved to build an earthly representation of paradise. From the farthest reaches of his empire (which included parts of present-day India, Afghanistan, Pakistan and Bangladesh), he summoned architects, stonemasons and artisans—some 20,000 of them—who labored for more than two decades on the royal mausoleum.

Because Islamic belief forbids graphic representations of the divine, this vision of eternity is evoked, not stated; it is a tale told in geometry and proportion, symmetry and grace. Clad entirely in white marble, the Taj Mahal rises more than 200 ft. over a garden with four canals representing the Four Rivers of Paradise, which are said to flow with water, milk, wine and honey. The interior walls of the building are inlaid with black stone calligraphy, citing verses from the Koran on the afterlife. The elegant white dome resembles a giant pearl floating above the building's four minarets, recalling the Prophet Muhammad's vision of the throne of God as a pearl surrounded by four pillars. It is on just such a throne that Shah Jahan believed God would sit in judgment of him, before welcoming him into paradise—and the arms of the wife he had lost. ∎

Legend Shah Jahan ("Ruler of the Universe") and wife Mumtaz Mahal were unusually close for an Islamic royal couple of the 17th century: she advised him on matters of state. Deposed by his son, the Shah never built the splendid tomb for himself that was to occupy a site across the river from the Taj Mahal.

Schloss Neuschwanstein

Füssen, Bavaria • 1886
Christian Jank, architect

Once upon a time there lived in Bavaria a young prince who read too many fairy tales and had too much money— a circumstance guaranteed to alarm royal ministers and excite royal architects. The time was the 1860s, the raging height of the Romantic movement, when *The Sorrows of Young Werther* and the operas of Richard Wagner stirred German souls. The prince was Ludwig, of the house of Wittelsbach, who became King Ludwig II of Bavaria at only 18, in 1864. And the result of his obsessions was a series of madly romantic, madly lavish, madly expensive castles, the most famed of which is Schloss Neuschwanstein, near Oberammergau. Did we mention that this royal builder is known to history as "Mad" King Ludwig?

Sadly, upon becoming King, Ludwig did not live happily ever after. His ministers, fed up with his extravagances, had him declared insane in 1886, when he was only 40, and placed him under *schloss* arrest on one of his less fanciful estates. A doctor was assigned to care for him; three days later both doctor and patient drowned in a nearby lake. The deaths were never explained. Today, more than a century later, Ludwig's buildings cast the kind of spell that even ministers understand: they are a major tourist attraction for Bavaria.

If Neuschwanstein looks familiar, that's because it's the template for Walt Disney's knockoffs at Disneyland and Disney World. Like the Disney versions, the interior is not finished: Ludwig's ministers pulled the plug after 17 years of construction, before the castle was completed. Then again, Neuschwanstein, like Disneyland, was never intended to be more than a stimulating stage set: architect Christian Jank was a theater designer. It's pure Bavarian hokum—Schlock Neuschwanstein— but there's glory in this madness. ∎

80 rms, great vus Ludwig was dethroned before the interior of Schloss Neuschwanstein (the New Swan's Stone) could be finished, but some rooms came near completion. Above is the three-story Throne Room, adorned in Byzantine style, complete with inlaid camels on the floor. Ludwig's lavish visions kept an army of builders, artists and craftsmen employed at royal expense.

The couple in the mural below, seen behind an elaborately carved wooden piece, are composer Richard Wagner's medieval lovers, Tristan and Isolde. The castle also includes a lavish Singers' Hall, inspired by Wagner's *Die Meistersinger;* Ludwig befriended the Romantic composer as a young man, and the castle is in many ways an attempt to turn Wagner's fantasies into reality.

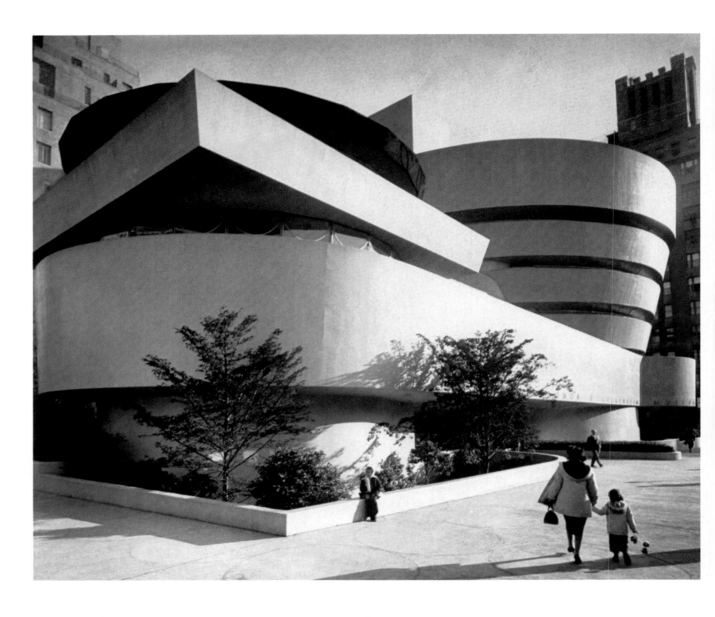

Solomon R. Guggenheim Museum

New York City • 1959
Frank Lloyd Wright, architect

When copper magnate Solomon R. Guggenheim decided to build a lavish, namesake palace in New York City to show off his impressive collection of modern art, he turned to Frank Lloyd Wright, the cranky iconoclast of 20th century American architecture. It was an odd choice: Wright famously hated cities, and he hated New York City with special bile. The prophet of the Prairie Style immediately began lobbying to have the museum moved away from Guggenheim's designated site—a choice block on Manhattan's Fifth Avenue, facing Central Park—and into the park itself, where the natural environment

would better suit his "organic" style. After losing that argument, Wright came up with an inspired act of nose-thumbing: he resolved to rebel pointedly against the city's right-angled, linear grid (as well as the constricted architectural establishment that resided within it) by designing a circular building.

For what would be his last major work, Wright dreamed up an "optimistic ziggurat"—a sloping white spiral that would guide visitors along a quarter-mile-long ramp, along which artworks would hang on walls that leaned outward at the same angle as an artist's easel. A glass dome at the spiral's summit would bathe

the exhibits in natural light. The design, which Wright tweaked for 17 years, was so unusual that a construction firm specializing in parking garages and freeway ramps was retained to build it.

When artists learned what Wright had wrought, they rebelled. Willem de Kooning, Robert Motherwell and Franz Kline signed an open letter to the museum's directors, protesting that Wright's "curvilinear slope indicates a callous disregard for the fundamental rectilinear frame of reference." Wright retorted that no such frame existed, except when cultivated "by callous disregard of nature, all too common in your art."

Wright was wrong, and the artists were right: the museum's walls curve; paintings don't. And the narrow width of Wright's sloping ramp forces viewers to stand closer to the paintings than many would like. But for Wright, these cavils were beside the point. He was trying to bring visitors into a more intimate relationship with art than most museums offered and also to make them look beyond the collection to the world around them—or, at least, the design around them. And as many visitors have noticed, it is perhaps not an accident that Wright's building, which is ostensibly dedicated to showcasing the best of modern art, has a glaring void at its center. ■

Sydney Opera House

Sydney, Australia • 1973
Jorn Utzon, architect

What the Eiffel Tower is to Paris, the Opera House is to Sydney: beloved icon, skyline tattoo, required photo-op. In its trademark interlocking white shells, observers have seen a giant armadillo, oysters and the pointed helmets of Spanish conquistadors. But architect Jorn Utzon says his design was inspired by the simple act of peeling an orange: the 14 shells of the building, if combined, would form a perfect sphere.

In 1957, Utzon, then 39, was virtually unknown outside his native Denmark when his entry in the design contest for the new Opera House was singled out by one of the judges, Eero Saarinen, who called it a work of genius and declared he could not endorse any other choice. Utzon's complex structure confounded the engineers who built it. They estimated the structure would cost $10 million and require three years' building time; they were only off by $40 million and 13 years. Long before the building was finished, Utzon was. Branded extravagant by cost-conscious politicians, he was officially given the sack in 1966. When the Opera House was opened by Queen Elizabeth II in 1973, the architect was not invited to the ceremony, nor was his name mentioned.

But over time, Sydneysiders—and the world—fell in love with Utzon's vision. Perched dramatically on a peninsula thrusting into Sydney Harbor, its lofty shells are covered by 1 million creamy white tiles that reflect the colors of sunlight and water throughout the city. The building was named a UNESCO World Heritage Site in 2007. Yet at the time of his death, at 90 in 2008, Utzon had never seen his finished masterpiece. ∎

DALE BOYER—STONE—GETTY IMAGES

Guggenheim Bilbao

Bilbao, Spain • 1997
Frank Gehry, architect

Bang! When it opened in 1997, the Guggenheim Museum hit Bilbao, Spain, with the force of an architectural meteorite, one whose reverberations traveled around the world and are still registering. Here was an apparition in glass and half-shiny silver (titanium, actually), massively undulating, something that seemed at first glance to have been dropped from another cultural world between the gray townscape and the green hills that rise behind it. Not since Jorn Utzon's Sydney Opera House had a building so dramatically imposed itself on a city. On the river edge of a town planned in terms of axial beaux arts order, architect Frank Gehry, then 68, inserted a startlingly irregular building that defied every convention of axiality, including the right angle, of which there doesn't appear to be one, either inside his structure or out.

After a long slump, building design was in the forefront of culture once again. Gehry's spectacular edifice was a reveille for architects, pointing into the future and spelling the end of the smarty-boots, smirkingly facile historicism on which so much post-Modernist building was based—a quoted capital here, an ironic reference there. Insisting that the essence of building is structure and placemaking, the museum confronted the rethinking of structure and the formation of space with an impetuous, eccentric confidence. No "school of Gehry" will ever come out of it, any more than there could have been a "school" of Barcelona's Antonio Gaudí. And that's the idea: this building is both imitation-proof and liberating. ■

Bird's Nest Stadium

Beijing · 2008
Herzog & de Meuron, primary architects

Architecture buffs have been following the visionary designs of Swiss firm Herzog & De Meuron for years, and the entire world finally caught up with them in 2008, thanks to the firm's dazzling main stadium for the Summer Olympics in Beijing. The building is really two joined structures: a red concrete bowl nestles inside the outer, steel-cage "bird's nest," which was originally designed to support a retractable roof that was later removed from the plans. The crisscrossing steel spans that support the outer structure are woven around translucent panels that give the building what the architects call a "porous" openness; the idea, they say, emerged from their study of Chinese ceramics. ∎

Turning Torso Building

Malmo, Sweden · 2005
Santiago Calatrava, architect

Spanish architect Santiago Calatrava has been turning heads since he first began erecting spectacular suspended bridges all across Europe in the 1980s. But he outdid himself with this spectacular tower in Malmo, when he managed to turn an entire 54-story skyscraper upon its axis. Here is a building that utilizes the full panoply of modern tools to close the door on 20th century design and offer a bold glimpse into the future of architecture. Calatrava, who is an artist and engineer as well as architect, modeled the skyscraper after his sculpture of a human body titled *Twisting Torso;* many of his buildings begin in his artworks, he has said. The building is 623 ft. (190 m) high; the primary tower is divided into nine segments of five stories; each story assumes a pentagon shape, with rooms clustered (like pieces of pie, it is sometimes said) around a central vertical core that holds utilities and elevators. Each story is rotated slightly from the one beneath it, and the top floor is rotated precisely 90° from the first story. An exterior mast, seen on the right, provides additional support and stability. ■

Where We Worship

Angkor Wat, Cambodia
*Begun under Khmer ruler Suryavarman II
in the 12th century, the vast temple complex,
nearly a mile long, was first sacred to Hindus
and is now a Buddhist shrine.*

The Tholos

**Delphi, Greece · 380-360 B.C.
Theodorus the Phocian, architect**

Zeus, resolved to find the center of the world, released two sacred eagles from the ends of the earth. The place where they met, a spring on the southern slopes of Mount Parnassus, was deemed to be the omphalos—the navel of the earth. It was here, in Delphi, that the ancient Greeks built a temple to Apollo (on what may have been an earlier Mycenaean cult site) in the 8th century B.C. Greeks seeking divine guidance would journey from all the city-states to Delphi, climbing 2,000 ft. to visit the Oracle, where a priestess would inhale the intoxicating vapors that issued from a cave on the site and answer questions in cryptic verse. Sadly, the Oracle's cave is lost to history; archaeologists believe it may have been covered by landslides.

Because Delphi was sacred to all Greeks, the site was nominally independent (in truth, control of the site changed hands among several city-states many times over the centuries) and thus it features a striking variety of Greek architectural styles. Treasury buildings to house donations were built in the Ionic and Doric styles of the Siphnians and Athenians, respectively. The Chians erected an altar of contrasting black and white marble; its stoa (porch) had seven fluted columns, each cut from a single stone.

At left is the Tholos, part of the Athena Pronaia sanctuary complex, the gateway to Delphi. It is believed to have been dedicated to the earth goddess, Gaia. The Roman architect and engineer Vitruvius, writing in the 1st century B.C., cited Theodorus the Phocian as its architect. Classically symmetrical, it consisted of 20 Doric columns encircling a group of 10 Corinthian columns, all crowned with a dome. ■

Hagia Sophia

Istanbul, Turkey • A.D. 537
Isidore of Miletus and Anthemius of Tralles, architects

One of the world's great witnesses of history, Hagia Sophia (Divine Wisdom) straddles cultures, empires, faiths and continents. For 1,000 years it was Christianity's foremost church; for 500 years it was one of Islam's chief mosques. Desanctified in the 1930s, it endures as a museum. It is built squarely upon one of civilization's fault lines, high on a hill in Istanbul, formerly Byzantium, formerly Constantinople. Look east, and you see the Bosporus, where Asia and Europe collide. Look west, and you see boats plying the Sea of Marmara, which links Istanbul to the Mediterranean. Look inside the doors of the great edifice, and you are peering into another dimension: time. This building was 1,000 years old when St. Peter's was built in Rome. It was 600 years old when the spires of Chartres Cathedral survived a devastating fire. One of the great functioning relics of the Roman Empire, it was built by the Emperor Justinian beginning in A.D. 532, some 80 years after Constantinople was founded as the capital of Rome's eastern realm by the Emperor Constantine, who made Christianity the official religion of the empire. Some 11,000 stonemasons labored to complete the structure in five years. "O Solomon, I have excelled thee!" Justinian is said to have exclaimed when the task was done.

The wonder of Hagia Sophia is its mighty dome: 107 ft. in diameter, its circular base is pierced by 40 windows, which seem to make the dome float in the clouds, suspended in the air. The two Greek architect-engineers who built it solved intricate geometric challenges in managing to support a huge circular dome upon a square base, attaching exterior half-domes to bear part of its weight, much like the flying buttresses of Gothic cathedrals.

The fault lines beneath the building are more than fanciful; it has withstood dozens of major earthquakes, the first of them while Justinian was still living, in 558. The great dome collapsed, and the Emperor ordered it rebuilt—with the dome raised 20 ft. higher. Desanctified by religion but ennobled by time, Hagia Sophia endures, surviving a bomb set off in its nave by Kurdish terrorists in 1994 and an earthquake that killed 17,000 in 1999. ■

Survivor For almost 1,000 years Constantinople reigned as the capital of Rome's eastern empire, which became the Byzantine Empire, but in 1453 Sultan Mehmet II conquered the city for Islam. The tolerant ruler preserved Hagia Sophia from desecration, saving its historic mosaics by plastering over them. Muslims erected four minarets around the building and placed a crescent moon on the dome, above, when they sanctified it as a mosque. Below, Islamic and Christian motifs clash within the building.

Potala Palace

Lhasa, Tibet • 1645-94
Architects unknown

Potala Palace, the most striking example of classic Tibetan architecture, is one of the few symbols of Tibetan nationalism that has survived the ongoing cultural purge by the Chinese, who have occupied the country since 1950. As befits the crowning jewel of a mountain kingdom, Potala ("Sacred Place") Palace sits on a high ridge more than 10,000 ft. above sea level, surrounded by hills that ring a vast plain. Its site has been the home of Tibet's kings and monks since the 7th century.

In 1645, the fifth Dalai Lama commissioned the first section, the White Palace, to commemorate the return of the Tibetan capital to the nearby city of Lhasa. After his death in 1682, a second section (the Red Palace) was built on top of the first. The completed structure towers 13 stories over the crest of the Marpo Ri (Red Hill) ridge and stretches almost a quarter-mile from north to south. Civil affairs were conducted in the lower White Palace, while religious matters were the province of the Red Palace above: in independent Tibet, spiritual authority trumped temporal power.

Reports of Lhasa and the palace reached European ears in the form of fables of a mythical Asian kingdom, Shangri-la. British photographer John Claude White astounded the world when he released the first pictures of the palace in 1904. Vast on every scale, the structure, now a museum, encloses more than a quarter-million square feet, contains some 1,000 rooms and is home to more than 200,000 statues and other artworks. ∎

St. Mark's Basilica

Venice • 1063-94
Architect unknown

Backdrop to millions of tourist pictures and prized perch for a piazza full of pigeons, St. Mark's Basilica is one of Europe's most historic structures, a living link to the days of the Crusades and to the emergence of the great merchant city-state of Venice as an imperial power. Originally a simple brick ducal chapel, it grew into one of the great symbols of Venice's wealth and influence after the body of St. Mark (San Marco) was smuggled out of Egypt by two Venetian traders in 1094 and placed within.

The building borrows elements from different cultures and eras—Byzantine, Romanesque, Gothic, Oriental, Renaissance—and yet achieves a unity all its own. Some of its treasures were not borrowed but pillaged: the four bronze horses that stand over the cathedral's portal were looted from Constantinople in 1204 in the Fourth Crusade. Cast in the 4th century A.D., either in Greece or Rome, they mark both Venice's rise to power and its decline: after Napoleon conquered Venice in 1797, ending its independence, he shipped the horses to Paris. They were returned after his downfall in 1815. Endangered by pollution, the original bronzes were put into storage in the late 1970s; those seen here above the central doorway are copies.

The real glory of St. Mark's can be found within its walls, indeed on its walls: they are covered in more than an acre of rich, shimmering mosaics, derived from the Byzantine tradition. Greek artisans were brought to Venice to create the mosaics, whose individual pieces, or tesserae, are made of gold, marble and the luminous glass for which the city has been known for centuries. ■

BENAINOUS—VANDEVILLE—GAMMA

Chartres Cathedral

Chartres, France • 1020-1260
Architects unknown

Swedish filmmaker Ingmar Bergman introduced *The Seventh Seal,* his 1957 film set in the Middle Ages, by recalling the story of the great cathedral Nôtre Dame du Chartres: "There is an old story of how the cathedral of Chartres was struck by lightning and burned to the ground. Then thousands of people came from all points of the compass, like a giant procession of ants, and together they began to rebuild the cathedral on its old site. They worked until the building was completed —master builders, artists, laborers, clowns, noblemen, priests, burghers. But they all remained anonymous, and no one knows to this day who built the cathedral."

Indeed, part of the enduring appeal of Europe's great Gothic cathedrals is their backstory: the massive structures arose across northern Europe in a frenzy of devotion. Here was an age when new technologies fused with religious passion, and to build was to pray: between 1170 and 1270, some 80 cathedrals and 500 major churches were built in France alone.

So lasting is the spell of these sacred spaces that centuries later, many cathedrals—St. Patrick's and St. John the Divine in Manhattan, the National Cathedral in Washington—were still being built on the Gothic template. Yet there is a whiff of the modern in the Gothic style: it marries form to function. The technical breakthroughs that create its soaring, aspirational quality are in plain view: the pointed Gothic arch, stronger and able to bear more weight than its rounded Romanesque predecessor; the stone rib vaults that ground the 121-ft.-tall ceilings; the flying buttresses that support the high walls on the outside, creating the unprecedented, spacious height of the interior. Freed from bearing loads, the inner walls seem to disappear, replaced by enormous windows, stained-glass artworks that suffuse the nave with otherworldly hues. The effect? Liftoff.

The masterminds of the Gothic style were itinerant stonemasons—at once artists, architects and engineers— who moved across Europe, sharing their expertise via the apprentice system. How the cathedral's cascade of fusions—between secular and sacred, art and science, mystic and mason, peasant and noble—must have appealed to Bergman, whose films limn a world of alienated, isolated souls, stripped of vision and purpose. ∎

Aspiring Chartres Cathedral is the latest of a series of churches and temples that have been built on its site: religious observances here date to the time of the Druids, before Christianity came to France. In 1194 a Romanesque church occupied the site, and two great spires were being added as an entry portal. The church burned down, but the bases of the spires stood, and the townspeople erected much of the new cathedral in a span of only 20 to 30 years, making it more focused in design than most Gothic churches, which can reflect stylistic evolutions that span centuries. However, Chartres' west front, right, does reflect two different periods: the unadorned right spire dates from the late 12th century; the far more ornate left spire was completed in 1513.

The building's flying buttresses, above, are one of the engineering innovations of the Gothic style. By bearing the weight of the roof away from the interior walls, these stone trusses allow space for the lofty stained-glass windows that are among the great treasures of Chartres.

Mont St. Michel

Normandy, France • 11th century
William of Volpiano, architect (*La Merveille*)

Pagan legends held that the rocky crag off France's northern coast was where the souls of the dead congregated. But for Aubert, bishop of nearby Avranches in the 8th century, the promontory was a place to meditate. One day the Archangel Michael appeared to Aubert and commanded him to build a church on the site, which becomes an island at high tide. The idea was madness, Aubert replied. But Michael persisted, appearing before Aubert two more times, even tapping him on the head for emphasis.

The small chapel that Aubert began in the year 708 blossomed, through the centuries, into a complex of churches, monasteries, convents and fortifications—jammed every which way onto an island less than 1 sq. mi. in area. As more buildings were added, earlier structures became the foundations for newer edifices. Beginning in the year 966, Benedictine monks completely encircled the natural outcropping of rock that dominated the island with a series of dormitories and chapels, thus raising a level platform to the 200-ft. summit.

In the 11th century, a new monastery church, a masterpiece appropriately named *La Merveille* ("the Marvel"), was perched atop the island. Throughout the Middle Ages, Mont St. Michel became both a place of pilgrimage and an unassailable strategic redoubt in wartime. What armies could not do, however, ideologues could: the monks were evicted during the French Revolution, and Mont St. Michel became a prison. It was not until 1966 that men of God were welcomed back to the place where an angel and a bishop once contended. ■

St. Basil's Cathedral

Moscow, Russia • 1561
Postnik Yakolev, architect

Fresh from his 1552 victory over the Mongols at Kazan, Czar Ivan IV (the Terrible) ordered a new church to be built outside the gates of the Kremlin, where all Moscow could see it. In designing the Cathedral of the Intercession, now St. Basil's, architect Postnik Yakolev borrowed Romanesque, Gothic and Renaissance motifs and topped off his church with a uniquely Russian twist: a bouquet of nine wondrous domes, each a different size, shape and color from the others. Napoleon ordered the church burned down when he retreated from Moscow in 1812; his freezing troops failed to do so. Joseph Stalin considered demolishing St. Basil's to make room for a subway station. When his chosen architect balked, Stalin relented, but he dispatched the man to the Gulag in revenge. A different menace now imperils the Russian Orthodox landmark: shifting soil beneath it threatens its stability. Engineers are exploring ways to save a holy place that was built by one of history's greatest tyrants—and that two others tried, but failed, to destroy. ∎

Basilica of St. Peter

St. Peter's Square, Vatican City • 1450-1626
Donato Bramante, primary architect

The millions of tourists who pass through the doors of the Basilica of St. Peter each year are drawn by a trinity of reasons. Hierarchy plays a part: this is the primary church of Roman Catholicism, oldest and largest of Christian religions. Art and history are here as well: filled with the sublime works of Italy's High Renaissance, St. Peter's is home to Michelangelo's moving *Pietà* and hundreds of other treasures. Finally, visitors come to marvel at the sheer scale and grandeur of the structure. It is Christendom's largest church, and should any doubter question its primacy, plaques marking the sizes of other churches are set in its marble floors for purposes of comparison.

Indeed, every aspect of St. Peter's is a bit outsized: it's small wonder why Protestant reformers railed against its excesses. It took 176 years to complete (1450-1626), and its designers are a Renaissance all-star team. Donato Bramante, one of its first architects, handed the baton to Raphael, and it ended up in the hands of Michelangelo. Along the way the shape of the church changed from a Greek cross, with four equal sides branching off a central dome, to a Latin cross, with a single, dominant, long nave. Outside, the arms of Gianlorenzo Bernini's tapering, colonnaded entry plaza (1667) seem to open and welcome visitors in an embrace; it is one of the world's finest arrival spaces. To pray within the great church's walls is to touch history. Here St. Peter was martyred. Here, after embracing Christianity, the Emperor Constantine first erected a basilica in the 4th century A.D. And here the Pope celebrates his church's most sacred annual observances. Here, present and past are as one. ∎

Notre Dame du Haut

Ronchamp, France • 1954
Le Corbusier, architect

The Swiss-born French architect Charles-Edouard Jeanneret, who dubbed himself Le Corbusier, was an unlikely choice to design the Catholic church in the French village of Ronchamp: he was a lifelong atheist and socialist. Perhaps its history inspired him. A destination for religious pilgrims since the 13th century, the hilltop was the site of a heroic last stand by French Resistance fighters in 1944, who were wiped out when German troops blew up the church in which they had taken refuge after a 10-week battle.

Le Corbusier began by ordering that the shards of the old church be collected—those broken stones would be worked into his design. Atop 10-ft.-thick walls that are fit for a fortress, he placed a curved roof that seems to billow in the wind, evoking both the contours of a French nun's habit and the profile of a bird about to take flight. From the exterior, the building is a different shape on each side—while inside, small irregularly placed windows project onto the white walls a shifting, sliding drama of light and shadow. At Our Lady on High, the man who was one of Modernism's champions of the rational revealed his soul: here, geometry gives way to poetry, mathematical precision to intuitive lyricism, angular purity to a flowing surrealism. ■

La Sagrada Família

Barcelona · 1883-present
Antonio Gaudí, architect

In an era when intellectuals and their theories dominated architecture, Antonio Gaudí was, above all, an acolyte of emotion. And the project he was most passionate about was the Temple Expiatori de la Sagrada Família (Expiatory Church of the Holy Family), in Barcelona. Winning the commission in 1883 because one of the builders had dreamed he would hire an architect with blue eyes, Gaudí aimed to build Europe's tallest church, with a soaring Art Nouveau design.

A zealous Catholic, Gaudí created a visionary—almost hallucinatory—structure. Its vertiginous towers seem to melt and swell like candles in the Spanish sun, while its encrusted layers of sculpture appear to sprout from the stone. Gaudí crafted a dizzying array of curving, open-ended forms that computer calculations would confirm, decades later, to be structurally perfect. Gaudí's masterpiece is now about half complete and is not expected to be finished until the middle of the 21st century. ∎

Case Study House No. 22 *Architect Pierre Koenig's 1960 wide-open masterpiece is cantilevered and swathed in glass to highlight its best feature: a spectacular view of Los Angeles*

Where We Live

House of the Vettii

Pompeii, Italy • 1st century A.D. • Architects unknown

"You could hear the shrieks of women, the wailing of infants, and the shouting of men," wrote Pliny the Younger, the most eloquent eyewitness to the explosion of Mount Vesuvius in the summer of A.D. 79. "Many ... imagined there were no gods left, and that the universe was plunged into eternal darkness for evermore." But where Pliny found darkness, history has found light: the eruption of Vesuvius preserved the buildings of Pompeii, a Roman provincial capital, in a protective blanket of ash and lava.

The courtyard shown here is from the House of the Vettii, named for two brothers whose signet rings were found within it; they appear to have been former slaves who later prospered as wine merchants. The enclosed courtyard, with fountains and statues of marble and bronze, was designed to be visible from the street, the better to display the owners' affluence. The home's rounded arches, tiled roofs, colorful frescoes and colonnaded courtyard make up a template for domestic architecture in temperate climes; its echoes can be found in buildings ranging from Moorish Spain to colonial Ecuador to today's Palm Springs. ■

Villa Rotonda

Vicenza, Italy • 1560s • Andrea Palladio, architect

An architectural riddle: What common spirit underlies English castles, American public buildings, Swiss railroad stations, Spanish libraries, Tuscan villas and Canadian hotels? The answer: All these buildings echo the influence of the Greeks and Romans, as filtered through the genius of Renaissance man Andrea Palladio, the 16th century Italian architect whose reinterpretations of the design legacies of antiquity have been the dominant language of architecture for the past 400 years. The power, uplift, balance and simplicity of Palladio's work are best captured in Villa Rotonda, the country home he designed in the 1560s for Paolo Almerico, a retired cleric.

Crowning a hill in the Italian countryside, Villa Rotonda seems poised between heaven and earth.

The gentle, graceful curve of its dome (inspired by the Pantheon) reaches skyward, while the four identical porticoes that flank it on each side anchor the house firmly to the ground. Its scale is just grand enough to inspire yet restrained enough not to overpower. Palladio rotated the corners of the house 45° away from the four points of the compass, so that each section would receive some sunlight throughout the day. Beneath the dome, the central hall is adorned with pastel frescoes and gives way to square, severe rooms with high ceilings. A master of proportion, Palladio took the design vernacular of a pagan age—pediments, porticoes and pillars, domes, arches and octagons— and gleaned from its clean Euclidean symmetries the blueprints for an Age of Reason. ■

Prague Castle

Prague • 10th to 18th centuries • Various architects

Prague Castle, the soaring complex of fortifications, palaces, cathedrals and government offices that crowns the Czech capital's highest hilltop, is a glorious patchwork of styles and eras, reflecting the many centuries over which it was built. Bohemian princes lived and ruled here, as did Holy Roman Emperors, Nazi generals and Soviet stooges. Begun as a fort by Prince Boleslav in 973, when the Czech nation was first united, it was expanded to enclose a nearby cathedral built earlier by King Wenceslas, on left. By the time Charles IV, King of Bohemia, was crowned Holy Roman Emperor in 1355, the complex had grown to include more churches, a palace and a library. From here, Charles presided over a golden age in which Prague became the political and cultural center of the Continent. His successors added gates, gardens, towers and courtyards in a dizzying array of styles: Gothic, Baroque, Romanesque, Rococo. This layering yielded not architectural chaos, but rather a rich, unified repository of Czech culture: a home for the nation's soul. ∎

Monticello

Charlottesville, Virginia • 1772
Thomas Jefferson, architect

When still in his 20s, Thomas Jefferson scaled an 800-ft. mountain that his recently deceased father had willed to him and was transfixed by the majestic view it afforded of the Rivanna Valley below. "How sublime to look down into the work-house of nature," he would later write, "to see her clouds, hail, snow, rain, thunder all fabricated at our feet!" He decided then and there he would build his home on this peak. Taking for its name an Italian phrase that translates loosely as "Little Mountain," he called it Monticello.

For the next six decades, Jefferson would not stop designing, building, demolishing and remodeling the home that he thought of as his life's work. "Architecture is my delight, and putting up and pulling down one of my favorite amusements," he admitted in his 50s. The result, Monticello, is as hard to pin down as the genius who designed it: the man who hailed liberty but held slaves; the radical egalitarian who was also a landed aristocrat; the thinker whose life was marked by a constant battle between idealism and practicality.

Yet Jefferson the architect's sense of balance resolved these opposing impulses into unified eloquence. On Monticello's West Portico, a montage of straight-lined triangles, rectangles and octagons is arrayed beautifully against the gentle curves of stone pillars, balustrades, round windows and the fine dome that caps the hilltop. "I am as happy nowhere else," Jefferson once wrote, "and all my wishes end, where I hope my days will end, at Monticello." On July 4th, 1826—50 years to the day after the signing of the Declaration of Independence and within hours of the passing of his lifelong rival and eventual friend, John Adams—Thomas Jefferson got his wish: he died in his bed at the home he had spent his life building. ∎

Hearst Castle

San Simeon, California • 1919-42
Julia Morgan, architect

From boyhood, future media mogul William Randolph Hearst loved camping out at the 250,000-acre wilderness that his father, mining millionaire George Hearst, owned near San Simeon on the California coast, midway between Los Angeles and San Francisco. But the grownup William decided that he preferred ceilings and beds to tents and sleeping bags. So he cabled his architect, Julia Morgan: "I would like to build a little something."

The problem: Hearst couldn't think little. After being kicked out of Harvard (for presenting his professors with chamber pots that had their names engraved inside), he took over a San Francisco newspaper his father had won gambling and parlayed it into a media empire that included newspapers, magazines, radio stations, a wire service and two film studios. Hearst's fortune and his imperial pretensions marched in lock-step. The first plan for La Cuesta Encantada (The

Enchanted Hill) was for a few simple bungalows; these became three Italianate villas, which in turn became guest houses to an immense (60,000 sq. ft., 115 rooms) mansion, Casa Grande, based on a Spanish cathedral. Inside were thousands of paintings, statues, tapestries, carpets and antiques that Hearst's buyers had pillaged … uh … amassed from around the world.

An army of workers labored for more than 20 years in pursuit of Hearst's ever receding goal: to create an edifice as vast as his ego. During the Depression, it was the single largest nongovernment construction project in California. Work finally stopped in 1942, when Hearst was mired in debt. At his death in 1951, Hearst Castle remained unfinished. The Hearst family donated the estate to California in 1957; it remains unfinished to this day. Yes, it's a wild, clashing farrago of nostalgia, megalomania and random architectural styles, but it does achieve its purpose: it makes your jaw drop. ■

Fallingwater

Stewart Township, Pa. • 1939
Frank Lloyd Wright, architect

The most famous—and, arguably, the most beautiful—house built in the 20th century is a fusion of rock, water and concrete, of nature's undulating lines and the architect's geometrical planes, where the handiwork of geology and man meet in easy, eternal balance. This is what Frank Lloyd Wright meant by "organic" architecture.

In the mid-1930s, as Wright's career was scraping bottom, he was hired by Pittsburgh department-store impresario Edgar J. Kaufman to design a weekend retreat at his dairy farm in the Pennsylvania countryside. The result, well, made a splash: Fallingwater swiftly rose to worldwide renown upon its completion in 1939. But it's more than hype that makes people love this building: Fallingwater is Wright's masterpiece. From the outside, it hovers weightlessly over the waterfall. Within, Wright evokes the feel of the surrounding forest, with rooms that open like clearings, windows that pull outdoor spaces inside, and horizontal planes of concrete that bind building and site together.

As usual, Wright's design is least perfect where least visible. He was, at best, indifferent about engineering, and Kaufman spent the rest of his life worrying that not enough structural steel had been used in the heavy, cantilevered concrete terraces, which began to crack even before the structure was completed—though Wright's apprentices, without the master's knowledge, had specified twice as much steel as he had called for. Sure enough, in the 1990s engineers declared that the building was about to fall into the creek (and might have decades earlier, but for the extra steel), and it underwent an emergency, $11 million makeover. But this building's glories more than make up for its engineering flaws. Wright spent decades proclaiming his genius; Fallingwater makes his case better, without saying a word. ■

rnsworth House

Illinois · 1951 · Ludwig Mies van der Rohe, architect

fter a shower, Edith Farnsworth stepped out of her bathroom—the only enclosed, private space in the open-plan glass house her friend Mies van der Rohe had designed for her—and fronted by a gaggle of Japanese tourists standing her transparent walls, snapping pictures. Such pitfalls of living in a Miesian masterpiece. Con-

sisting of sheer glass walls hung between two horizontal planes of marble, Farnsworth House is suspended 5 ft. above the Illinois soil by eight evenly spaced steel columns that evoke the elegant symmetry of a Greek temple. At night it is a floating rectangle of light, hovering over the grass—a breathtaking effect that the architect refused to spoil by adding curtains to his windows.

Farnsworth has greater problems than nosy sightseers. The glass walls make the home a hothouse in summer: only one window opens, and Mies didn't want his sleek lines ruined by air-conditioning machinery. In winter, the poorly insulated building freezes and the windows fog up. In spring, when the nearby Fox River spills over its banks, the house can be accessible only by canoe.

In 1972, the frustrated owners sold the 2,000-sq.-ft. house to British builder (and Mies acolyte) Lord Peter Palumbo, who painstakingly restored and preserved it. In 2003, this platonic ideal of a domicile was forever relieved of the need to accommodate the mundane concerns of human residents: Palumbo sold it to the National Trust for Historic Preservation, and it is now a museum. ∎

Eames House

Pacific Palisades, California • 1949 • Charles and Ray Eames, architects

World War II was won, and young American soldiers were returning home. So John Entenza, the owner and editor of *Arts & Architecture* magazine, commissioned a series of 24 new houses in the Los Angeles area to explore how to put roofs over the heads of millions of young families. Several ideas pioneered in these "Case Studies," such as the use of sliding glass doors to fuse indoor and outdoor space and the reversal of the traditional floor plan by placing the living room at the back of the home, away from the street, became standard features of 1950s hous-

ing. The home that best suited the era's emerging lifestyles was Case Study House No. 8, by husband and wife designers Charles and Ray Eames.

For their California home and workspace, the two chose parts available at any building supply vendor: standard 4-in., H-shaped columns; factory windows with X-trusses between them. They jazzed up this utilitarian façade with color panels in a geometric grid, recalling the paintings of Piet Mondrian. Inside, the home has few walls, allowing for a maximum of flexibility and spaciousness: it opened the doors of a million knockoffs. ■

Villa Mairea

Noormarkku, Finland • 1939 • Alvar Aalto, architect

He is a genius," Frank Lloyd Wright said, after seeing the work that brought Alvar Aalto fame in America, the Finnish Pavilion at the 1939 World's Fair in New York City. Like Wright, the Finn tried to meld Modernism's hard, technological edges with the softer, organic forms of nature. And as with Wright, one of Aalto's masterpieces is a small, private country home built for wealthy friends.

In 1937, Harry and Maire Gullichsen commissioned Aalto to build a retreat for them in a pine forest near the town of Noormarkku. They asked for a home that was both modern and classically Finnish, both elegant and unostentatious, both rustic and progressive. To square these circles, Aalto created a sort of domestic collage, a patchwork home that stitched together traces of Finnish farm architecture, Gothic churches and influences from as far afield as California and Japan. But a single theme resonates most: pine logs, wooden poles and steel posts covered in rattan or birch appear throughout Villa Mairea, evoking its forest setting, as well as the larger culture and landscape of Finland. Aalto was inspired by Wright: like Fallingwater's, Villa Mairea's floor plan is a series of flowing internal spaces that mimic branching forest paths. As a result, this architectural experiment is also a supremely open and livable space. ∎

American Iconoclast

His outsize persona may have been his single greatest creation, but Frank Lloyd Wright was the genius he claimed to be

Like his renowned Solomon R. Guggenheim Museum, a defiant circle thumbing its nose at Manhattan's right-angle grid—Frank Lloyd Wright wasn't made to fit in. He never earned a degree in architecture. He built only a handful of skyscrapers, the buildings with which many 20th century designers made their reputations. And almost alone among recent major architects, he hated cities, believing that mankind's utopian future lay in agrarian communes where structures and nature would be one.

Wright was a dyspeptic smart-aleck who referred to the International Style pioneered by his rival, Ludwig Mies van der Rohe, as "neither international nor a style" and challenged wealthy clients by ranting about "unnatural reservoirs of predatory capital." He was always itching to found a bona fide "movement"— Prairie Style, Organic Style, Usonian Style and so on— and his various autobiographies read more like manifestos than memoirs. He was vain, a crank in a purple cape who habitually lied about his age and often behaved like an aspiring cult leader—gathering around him small armies of acolytes to live communally at rustic compounds in Wisconsin and Arizona.

Yet Wright was not simply a poseur: he invented a new, uniquely American aesthetic that owed nothing to inherited European forms. Asked to name other architects who had influenced him, he replied, with his usual modesty, "None." Reading Emerson and Thoreau from an early age, Wright grew up believing that one man's vision of truth could reshape the world. In his early 20s, he set out to do just that, with (as he put it) "a hod of mortar and some bricks." Born in 1867, he apprenticed under the great Chicago architect Louis Sullivan (and amended his famous dictum, "Form follows function," to, "Form and function are one"). Wright established an early reputation building private homes in the suburbs of Chicago that were unlike any residences seen before.

From the outside, these houses were unusual, in a surprisingly unobtrusive way. Where boxlike, two- or three-story Victorian homes dominated their settings, Wright's long, low Prairie Style houses, all horizontal planes, blended harmoniously with their surroundings. "No house should ever be on a hill or on anything," he would say later. "It should be of the hill, belonging to it." The interiors of these homes were radically new: indoor rooms flowed seamlessly into outdoor spaces; tiny hallways opened onto vast, expansive chambers; natural light flowed from one part of the building to another during the day. From the first, Wright displayed an almost magical ability to manipulate space: stretching and compressing it, molding and bending it to his will.

When Wright's serene homes brought fame and success, he devoted himself to his working retreat in the Wisconsin countryside, where he had spent summers as a child. Called Taliesin (Welsh for "Shining Brow"), this 600-acre enclave became his home, studio, architecture school and farm. There he gathered family, students and admirers to live as a self-sustaining community, in strict conformance with his ideas about, well, pretty much everything: the fields were planted to yield crops based on the master's approved color scheme.

In 1916 Wright was awarded his first truly monumental commission, the Imperial Hotel in Tokyo, whose ingenious system of structural supports kept the hotel intact during a devastating 1923 earthquake that flattened almost all the buildings around it. The structure could not withstand the pressure of commercial redevelopment, however; it was demolished in 1968.

Tremors also rocked Wright's personal life. In 1909 he left his wife and children to take up with the wife of a client; she was in turn murdered (along with her two children and four of Wright's associates) by a disgruntled servant at Taliesin, who then burned the place to the ground. Taliesin was rebuilt, but bankruptcy, depression and ever shifting professional fortunes would plague Wright for the rest of his life.

The 1930s brought more Wright masterpieces, including Fallingwater, the brilliantly organic home in Pennsylvania, and the Johnson Wax headquarters in Racine, Wis., which LIFE magazine in 1938 compared to "a woman swimming naked in a stream … cool, gliding, musical in movement and manner." He also designed a second communal retreat, Taliesin West in Arizona, where he spent much of the rest of his life.

After World War II, Wright developed the Usonian Style, hoping to build attractive, inexpensive homes for middle-class Americans. But this visionary was no master of utility. The roofs of his buildings leaked more often than not, his creations were notoriously difficult (and expensive) to heat, and he regularly poured scalding contempt on clients who requested even minor changes in his designs. A control freak, he would argue with the owners of his homes over where the furniture (which he often designed) should be placed. When he died in 1959 (at 89), Wright—as he no doubt would have preferred—was both lavishly hailed and scornfully dismissed. In the years before his death, rival Philip Johnson snidely termed him "the best American architect of the 19th century." Maybe so—but it's telling that even Johnson's put-down includes an encomium. ∎

IMPERIAL HOTEL, TOKYO, 1916-22

Wright's masterwork was demolished in 1968. Of its Asian feel, he wrote, "I have sometimes been asked why I did not make the opus more 'modern' … there was a tradition there worthy of respect and I felt it my duty as well as my privilege to make the building belong to them [the Japanese] so far as I might."

TALIESIN EAST, WISCONSIN, 1925

Wright's interiors were made to order. He generally designed every element of the home: lights, chairs and desks, rug patterns and the colored insets in the windows (he even tried to design clients' clothing). The joined windows at left open up the view, while obscuring the corner of the house. Wright preferred to work with local stone, which he often left unfinished, as he sought to achieve an organic unity between site and structure.

TALIESIN WEST, ARIZONA, 1937

As with the Robie House, top right, which he designed decades before, Wright hid the windows beneath the roofline in this desert workshop, which is flooded with natural light in the daytime. Wright's students helped build the structure, pouring concrete over native stone placed in forms to create the walls. Redwood columns support the roof.

"I [had] to choose between honest arrogance and a hypocritical humility ... the world knows what I chose. " —FRANK LLOYD WRIGHT

ROBIE HOUSE, OAK PARK, ILL., 1909

The residence's cantilevered roofs and raised balustrades carefully shield it from the street and help disguise the enormous banks of windows that bring natural light into the home. Once inside, visitors find that the rather imposing exterior gives way to a sense of spaciousness and modern, streamlined glamour, created by the high ceilings, extensive windows and richly detailed woodwork. In the home's private rooms, the ceilings are quite low—Wright called the feel "democratic," but critics contend he was designing to fit his own rather diminutive (5 ft. 7 in.) size. The home's strong horizontal lines issue from Wright's conviction that a building should merge with its setting—in this case the flat landscape of the American Midwest. The building is now owned by the University of Chicago and is a National Historic Landmark.

JOHNSON WAX BUILDING GARAGE, RACINE, WIS., 1936

Wright echoed the lily-pad shapes of this office building's interior columns in its underground car park, where the streamlined curves of a late-'30s roadster look completely at home. The architect's early Prairie Style was angular, featuring long horizontal planes and severe right angles. Later in his career, Wright began to explore more fluid and fanciful forms, experiments that would culminate in the delicious spiral of New York City's Solomon R. Guggenheim Museum.

Where The
Arts Live

Teatro alla Scala

Milan • 1778 • Giuseppe Piermarini, architect

Opera lovers the world over, no matter their nationality, call one place their spiritual home: Milan's Teatro alla Scala, better known by its abbreviated name, La Scala. When the city's previous opera house, the Regio Ducal Teatro, burned down in the 1770s, the Austrian Empress Maria Theresa, then Milan's ruler, commissioned architect Giuseppe Piermarini to design a replacement. She underwrote the project by deeding the plot on which it would stand to local nobles who coveted private boxes in the theater, and then charging them a membership fee.

Piermarini designed an ornate façade (it took five versions before his work suited the over-the-top tastes of his patrons) with neoclassical arches and a pediment that depicts Apollo racing in his chariot. But it is the interior of La Scala that truly sings; it seems cozy and familiar, though it seats 1,800. Yet it is grand, as well: its horseshoe of six tiers of box seats surrounds the two-level Royal Box, which perches over the building's entrance,

directly opposite the stage, and draws the visitor's attention like a second, miniature proscenium.

An honor roll of great Italian composers—Donizetti, Bellini, Rossini and Verdi—has written for this stage. It was here that Verdi staged his first opera, *Oberto,* in 1839; he returned later in life, after a feud with management that kept him away for more than 20 years, to premiere his last masterpieces, *Otello* in 1887 and *Falstaff* in 1893.

For much of the 20th century, La Scala remained the private property of the titled families who owned its boxes, which were decorated with their heraldic coats of arms. The theater was flattened by an Allied bombing raid in World War II, but the Milanese so cherish La Scala that once the war ended they chose to rebuild it before any other structure in the city, even ahead of desperately needed housing and hospital facilities. The beloved theater's interior was remodeled in 2004, and if you suppose the result didn't create an uproar—well, you haven't attended too many operas in Milan. ■

Royal Albert Hall

London • 1871 • Francis Fowke and Henry Y.D. Scott, architects

The Royal Albert Hall is Britain's "village hall": within its elliptical walls, Olympic athletes contended, Winston Churchill spoke, Laurence Olivier performed Shakespeare, the Beatles sang, and J.K. Rowling read *Harry Potter* books to children. Despite its imperfect acoustics and feeble ventilation system (both of which were greatly improved by a 10-year renovation completed in 2004), the Albert ranks in the affections of Britons somewhere between Big Ben and Benny Hill.

The hall is the brainchild of Prince Albert, Queen Victoria's royal consort, who dreamed of creating what some detractors called "Albertopolis"—a cultural, scientific and academic city within a city that would continue to attract the international intelligentsia who had flocked to the great London Exhibition of 1851, which he strongly supported.

Using profits from the exhibition, Albert purchased an estate in Kensington, not far from the site of the famed Crystal Palace, and set about erecting his Xanadu, which he envisioned as a set of performance and exhibition spaces that would seat 30,000 spectators. He enlisted Henry Cole, who had assisted the Prince on several public works projects, as his adviser; Francis Fowke and Henry Y.D. Scott were the building's architects. Before the first stone could be laid, however, Albert died of typhoid fever in 1861. When the hall opened in 1871, its name was changed to honor its founder. Though funding woes reduced its size from Albert's grandiose plans, it still seats 7,000 listeners—a large size for a concert hall.

In the decades after the auditorium opened, the campus of cultural ferment that Albert envisioned blossomed all around it: the area is now home to the Imperial College of Science, Technology, and Medicine; the Royal College of Art; the Victoria and Albert Museum; the Science Museum; the Natural History Museum; and the Royal Geographical Society. So it's fitting that the Royal Albert Hall is crowned by an 800-ft. frieze that circles the building and is inscribed with these words: "This Hall was erected for the advancement of the Arts and Sciences and works of industry of all nations in fulfillment of the intention of Albert, Prince Consort." ∎

Louvre Museum

**Paris • 11th to 17th centuries
Various architects**

I.M. Pei, architect, pyramid • 1989

The Louvre Museum is a great living repository of French history. Long the Paris palace of France's kings, it bears the fingerprints of medieval monarchs, Renaissance architects, 17th century sculptors and the Emperors Napoleon I and III. Routinely described as the world's foremost museum, it is the home of the *Winged Victory of Samothrace,* the *Venus de Milo* and Leonardo's *Mona Lisa.* But since 1989 the Louvre's art and history have played second fiddle to its geometry: people can't stop talking about the pyramid.

In the early 1980s, French President François Mitterrand asked Sino-American architect I.M. Pei to reinvent the Louvre to accommodate the millions of visitors it attracts each year. Pei's visionary proposal: placing a huge glass pyramid smack in the middle of the historic edifice's central courtyard. The translucent structure would serve as an entry portal, funneling visitors (and natural light) underground into a modern entrance complex.

When Pei's plans were unveiled in 1984, Parisians reviled the pyramid. Here, they charged, was a slice of Modernism dropped with no concern for context into a hallowed site. Mitterrand was scoffingly branded "Mitterramses." And as for Pei: Well, why not revive the guillotine? But—*sacre bleu!*—the vast glass mass works. Its formal shape is of a piece with the French capital's neo-classical buildings and classical gardens. It offers visitors a memorable, efficient welcome. But the pyramid's true greatness lies in the sheer audacity of its conception. Eschewing the safe path of concealing a modern building within a shell designed to ape its surroundings, Pei argues with this startling juxtaposition that modern buildings can take their place alongside the finest of the past, if they offer a vision that is grand enough—and clear enough. ∎

Paris Opera

Paris • 1878 • Charles Garnier, architect

Composer Claude Debussy said it reminded him of a Turkish bathhouse. The London *Times* ventured that its architect, Charles Garnier, had perhaps "over-egged the pudding." Empress Eugénie, wife of its patron, Napoleon III, slighted Garnier's design: "What is this style? It isn't style. It's not Greek, not Louis XV, not Louis XVI." (His unfazed reply: "No. This is the style of the times. It is the style of Napoleon III, and you are complaining about yourself!") Call it what you will, in this case, nothing succeeds like excess: the Paris Opera is the world's most famous auditorium. Of course, it helps that this is a haunted house: the Palais Garnier, as it is also known, will always be the home of novelist Gaston Leroux's *Phantom of the Opera.*

Razzle-Dazzle 'Em Charles Garnier's façade is encrusted with ornament, including six types of limestone, 10 variations of marble, mosaic panels edged in gold leaf and gilded statues. Inside, Marc Chagall's radiant 1964 mural on the interior of the dome, below, is a welcome addition to the building.

The great theater is a lasting relic of a fleeting regime. It was commissioned by Napoleon III, the vainglorious nephew of Napoleon Bonaparte, in order to leave the stamp of his Second Empire on Paris. Garnier won an international contest to design the building in 1861, when he was only 32, but the elaborate structure wasn't completed until 1878, eight years after Napoleon III's fall. In its heyday, during Paris' Belle Epoque, Garnier's building well suited an audience that came as much to be seen as to see: its public spaces are nearly as extensive as its auditorium. The sumptuous grand marble staircase is made for sweeping ascents; the main foyer, above left, like a stage, is surrounded by boxes to offer the best view of the fascinating events unfolding below. Pity the poor soprano who had to compete for the attention of these stylish operagoers, reveling in the greatest show on earth: themselves. ∎

63

Pompidou Center

Paris • 1977
Richard Rogers and
Renzo Piano, architects

Art and Paris? The two belong together, like Hemingway and an aperitif. Yet Parisians were skeptical in 1969, when the French government decided to build a new center of art, music and learning intended to establish the City of Light as a cultural mecca for generations to come. The competition to design this center (which would eventually bear the name of French President Georges Pompidou) attracted the short list of that era's architectural superstars. So the design world was astounded when the plan of two young unknowns, Italian Renzo Piano and Briton Richard Rogers, was selected.

Their building was radical, futuristic and inside-out: a playful cacophony of periscope-style ducts and air vents, it looms against the Paris sky as if still under construction, while a tubular Plexiglas caterpillar of an escalator zigzags up its façade. Splashed in bright, primary colors, the structure resembles a comic-book drawing of a factory. The Pompidou Center put its then novel style—high tech—on the map. In part an insolent slap in the face of the Establishment that funded it, this museum-as-playhouse also argued that fine art didn't have to take itself seriously. Moreover, all were welcome here: the giddy escalator ride, with its great views of Paris, was free.

After its 1977 opening, the Pompidou Centre became the toast of Paris, drawing five times as many visitors each year as its builders had anticipated and necessitating a $120 million overhaul in 1997, during which the admission booth was moved to the foot of the escalator: the views of Paris are now reserved for paying customers. *Plus ça change!* ■

Getty Center

Los Angeles • 1997 • Richard Meier, architect

Perched on a sublime podium, a hilltop overlooking west Los Angeles, architect Richard Meier's magnificent Getty Center offers sweeping views of the metropolis, evoking comparisons to another shining city on a hill: this is indeed an American Acropolis. The museum complex pays tribute to the ancients in its ethos as well. The millions of visitors it attracts park their cars at its base and ascend to the site aboard a sleek monorail. The inescapable message: art is something above and beyond our mundane concerns, nobly elevated to a higher plane. In an era when many museums are actively seeking closer involvement with patrons' everyday lives, the Getty Center remains proudly aloof on its pedestal.

But there is no equivocating about the quality of
Meier's Modernist, six-building complex. The strong
Euclidean forms of the structures—domes, sweeping
curves, half-circles—are executed in gleaming, creamy
high-tech materials and Italian travertine. They are
quite reserved, but their reticence is apt, for their site
is so dazzling, this lily doesn't need much gilding. ◼

Jewish Museum of Berlin

Berlin • 2001 • Daniel Libeskind, architect

For almost two decades, Daniel Libeskind was the world's most respected virtual architect: though he had been an influential critic, writer, teacher and theorist since the early 1980s, he had never actually built anything. The project that drew the Polish-born American from the comfort of a podium to the turmoil of a building site was the Jewish Museum of Berlin.

This work came from the heart: 85 members of the Jewish architect's family were murdered by the Nazis, and his father barely survived a German concentration camp.

In 1988, when Berlin opened a competition to design a museum of Jewish history, Libeskind entered the fray. In announcing that his design had won (and admitting that it was deeply unconventional), the jury

Stabbed Inside the museum, windows slash through the walls at odd angles, like knife wounds. What seems random is not: Libeskind obtained from the German government a list of all the Berlin Jews who died in the Holocaust. He plotted their addresses on a map of the city and then drew lines to the places beyond the city limits where they were murdered or found refuge. These lines fixed the placement and angle of the windows, one of which points directly to Auschwitz.

Inside the building, three walkways trace the paths taken by Germany's Jews under Nazi rule—exile, death or (for a fortunate few) survival. Above is the building's fifth and final inner void, a dead end.

noted that "the obvious thing may have been to build a normal museum, had not one entry put forward a quite extraordinary, profound response."

When the museum opened (on the now unsettling date of Sept. 9, 2001), "extraordinary" and "profound" seemed understated. Outside, the building is a dissonant, zigzagging jumble of polygons wrapped in titanium and zinc. The shape may seem arbitrary, but its outline evokes the jagged shards of a shattered Star of David, a bolt of lightning or even the letter *S* as it appeared on the uniforms of Hitler's SS troops.

Throughout the museum a series of empty spaces puncture the walls, floors and ceilings. Libeskind calls these dimly lighted, raw concrete abscesses, in which no exhibits are presented, voids. They serve as silent, eloquent reminders that this museum's story, which enshrines the culture and history of Germany's Jews, comes to a horrifying, abrupt end: the voids direct our gaze to the culture that is no longer there, because it was wiped out; to the history that is no longer there, because it was erased; and to the people who are no longer there, because they were annihilated. ■

Bloch Building, Nelson-Atkins Museum

Kansas City • 2007
Steven Holl, architect

The main building of the Nelson-Atkins Museum of Art in Kansas City, Mo., on the right below, is a serene neoclassical structure from 1933. A stately terraced lawn with a sculpture garden pours down from the grand south entrance. When the museum decided to expand, most architects vying for the commission proposed building on the parking lot at the main building's rear, so as not to interfere with its grand façade. But American master Steven Holl, 63 in 2010, dared to suggest an addition that would cascade down the eastern edge of the museum's great lawn in a series of pavilions, translucent glass enclosures over gallery spaces located mostly underground. He called them lenses. Most of them would be oddly shaped, and at night they would glow from within. Holl placed the longest and most conventionally rectangular of his lenses at a perpendicular to the museum's rear façade, below. That created a square courtyard with a quiet reflecting pool where the parking lot used to be. As Holl puts it, he promised the museum's trustees that "the new will be as new as can be, but the old will be preserved." The luminous result doesn't merely mimic the classicism of the older museum building but reformulates it in 21st century terms. Most people see buildings as things made of steel and glass, wood and stone. Holl sees them first as things made of space and light. This time he comes as close as possible to working in pure light. ■

Cartier Foundation

Paris • 1994
Jean Nouvel, architect

The Pritzker Prize, awarded each year, is modern architecture's equivalent of the Nobel Prize or a knighthood in Britain, and as TIME art and architecture critic Richard Lacayo pointed out after French master Jean Nouvel was named the prizewinner for 2008: "It was always only a matter of time before the Pritzker Foundation said 'Arise, Sir Jean' to Nouvel, 62, who for decades has been one of the most closely followed architects in the world." Nouvel was already famous within the profession by 1981, when he was just 35. That was the year he won the commission for the Institute of the Arab World in Paris, whose most ingenious feature is a sunscreen created by thousands of steel-frame iris mechanisms. Arranged in Islamic tile patterns, they widen and contract in response to the sun. Architects talk sometimes about buildings having a skin. This one has pores.

How the outside comes inside would turn out to be one of Nouvel's great preoccupations. Transparency and paradox are others. Again and again he toys with the idea of buildings that seem to dematerialize, that play hide-and-seek as you approach them. His Cartier Foundation for Contemporary Art in Paris, completed in 1994, is a glass-walled structure that has another, free-standing glass wall set a few yards in front of it. You see the glass building behind a shimmering screen of glass that's constantly reflecting the street and sky. It's architecture as mirage. But its impact—as a translucent form seemingly composed only of glass, light and reflections—is very real. ∎

AMBROISE TÉZENAS—COURTESY OF FONDATION CARTIER

Thinking out of the Box

His early work drew scorn (and bullets); now Frank Gehry creates slippery masterpieces that make viewers swoon

Don't let Frank Gehry catch you calling him a deconstructivist or a populist or a post-Modernist or any of the other labels that have been tacked onto his work. And don't try either the characterization used since the dawn of his career by some of Gehry's most fervent admirers—as well as his most acerbic critics—that he is more an artist than an architect. "I don't call myself an artist," he insists. Instead, if you must call him something, call Frank Gehry, 81 in 2010, the world's most famous living architect. Even he couldn't argue with that.

Born Frank Goldberg in Toronto in 1929, Gehry grew up playing in the back of his grandfather's hardware store, fashioning miniature cities from scrap pieces of lumber and wood shavings. After moving to Los Angeles in the 1940s, the young Gehry drove a truck while he attended art classes at night school. He eventually enrolled in the architecture program at the University of Southern California and changed his name to Gehry, thinking that his Jewish surname might hurt his career prospects. "It's not something I would do today," he says with a hint of regret. "I'd like to change it back."

After stints at Harvard's Graduate School of Design and a year in Paris—during which he made pilgrimages to Europe's architectural treasures—Gehry returned to Los Angeles and began what promised to be an utterly conventional career, designing shopping malls and offices. On his own time, though, Gehry began sketching out radically offbeat design ideas.

In the late 1970s, Gehry made one of these ideas real: he converted a Dutch Colonial bungalow he and his wife had bought in Santa Monica into a wacky, off-kilter pastiche of raw construction materials, parapets and exposed structural elements. Neighbors howled (and someone fired a bullet into the house in apparent protest), but the architectural world was put on notice:

here was a major new talent of astonishing originality. Not long after, an emboldened Gehry cut his staff from 30 workers to three; struck up friendships with artists like Robert Rauschenberg, Jasper Johns and Claes Oldenburg; and began a lifelong habit of drawing inspiration from painting rather than from other architects.

In the early 1980s, Gehry was commissioned to help Los Angeles' Museum of Contemporary Art build a stopgap facility in an old police garage. Rather than disguise the existing structure, he wrapped it in a canopy of steel-framed chain-link fencing, setting up a fascinating tension between old and new. Critics dubbed Gehry's style "car crash" architecture—but as with a car crash, you couldn't look away.

In the late 1980s and early '90s, Gehry declared his independence from the angular, Euclidean design imperatives that had dominated architecture for thousands of years, and he embarked on an adventurous architecture of sweeping, sloping, curvilinear forms that had no precedent. Much of the work was made possible by using innovative computer software originally developed for aerospace designers.

Then, in 1997, came Bilbao. For the Guggenheim Museum's new annex in a rusting industrial city in Spain, Gehry created a sinuous, shimmering masterpiece that seemed a postcard from 2050—or beyond. In a single swooping stroke, Gehry, long an architects' cult figure, became a household name. On a roll, the architect wowed both critics and the public with undulating designs for the Experience Music Project in Seattle and the Walt Disney Concert Hall in Los Angeles.

Gehry throws a welcome curve ball into our cityscapes of Miesian rectangles. It's too early to tell whether his evanescent façades open a window into architecture's future or simply reflect a lone genius' quirky obsessions. But either way, the view is spectacular. ∎

"I'm interested in the game ... my clients have an object of desire in mind, and I try to realize it. I'm a geisha." —FRANK GEHRY

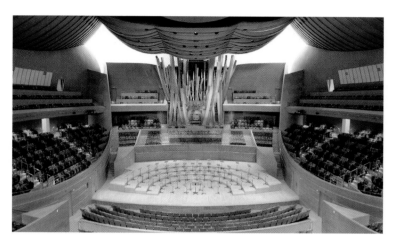

DISNEY CONCERT HALL, LOS ANGELES, 2003

Gehry began working on designs for a new home for the Los Angeles Philharmonic in the 1980s, but political and funding issues sidelined it for years. The building opened in the fall of 2003, to wide acclaim. Within the structure's slip-sliding-away exterior, left page, Gehry created a warm, symmetrical interior, near left, in cozy Douglas fir; the floor is covered with a sizzling floral-pattern carpet (not shown here) that is a nod to Lillian Disney, Walt Disney's widow, whose $50 million gift sparked the project. "I didn't want to create a pseudo-classical hall for classical music," Gehry said. Mission accomplished.

NORTON RESIDENCE, VENICE, CALIF., 1982-84

"Buildings under construction look nicer than buildings finished," Gehry once said, and he set out to prove his point with a series of homes he built in Venice and Santa Monica, Calif.; they feature such unfinished materials as plywood, concrete block and chain-link fencing. The Norton Residence in Venice appears to be a deconstructed series of modules from the outside, but the interior offers a gracious, sweeping—and surprisingly homey—refuge from the world. The free-standing cubicle looks out on the Pacific Ocean; it's also a witty nod to nearby lifeguard towers.

EXPERIENCE MUSIC PROJECT, SEATTLE, 2000

The architect claims the forms he used in this riotous, clashing museum of rock music were inspired by a heap of trash he found outside a guitar shop near his office in California.

Where We Assemble

Sacred Mosque, Mecca, Saudi Arabia
Islam's most sacred site is crowded with thousands of Muslims completing the hajj, or pilgrimage, each year

The Acropolis

Athens • 5th century B.C.
Ictinus and Callicrates, architects

All kinds of enterprises should be created which will provide an inspiration for every art and find employment for every hand," declared Pericles, the leading statesman of Athens, in the wake of the Greek city-state's triumph over the Persians at the Battle of Marathon in 490 B.C. Flush with victory, the Athenians resolved to undertake "such works as,

by their completion, will bring everlasting glory."

Before being driven off, the Persians had sacked Athens and destroyed the temples atop its Acropolis ("High Town"—a 10-acre mesalike plateau that rises hundreds of feet over the surrounding city). This strategic vantage point had been used as a fortification and a place of worship for eons. And this was where Athenians would create the greatest of Greek public works projects and the high-water mark of architectural and sculptural achievement in the ancient world.

Pericles entrusted the design to his friend, the gifted sculptor Phidias, and two architects, Ictinus and

Above it all Seen from above, the elevated Acropolis resembles a boat plowing through a sprawling Athens. The south porch of the Erechtheion, the Temple of Pallas Athena, is graced by a series of caryatids, right—female statues that bear the weight of the roof in place of columns. Those on the site are copies; the originals, to the continuing dismay of Greeks, remain with the Elgin marbles in the British Museum. Britain's Lord Elgin carted off a shipload of priceless artifacts early in the 19th century, ostensibly to preserve them from ongoing wars between Turkey and Greece.

Following the decline of the great city-states of Greece, the Romans treated the Parthenon reasonably well, and the former temple later served as both a Christian church and a mosque. The Turks cared for it poorly—they used the Parthenon as warehouse for explosives. The Venetians treated it worst of all—they bombed the Turks' ammunition dump while laying siege to Athens in 1687, setting off a huge explosion that wrecked the great structure.

TOP: YANNIS KONTOS—POLARIS; BOTTOM: GJON MILI—TIME LIFE PICTURES

Callicrates, who ordered 20,000 tons of marble to be quarried from nearby mountains. Ictinus was a master of entasis ("tension") and the optical tricks that can make subtly curved structures seem both light in weight and straight of line. In fact, there are almost no straight lines in the entire complex of temples and shrines at the Acropolis—although nearly every line appears so. Perfectly vertical columns, for example, would look deceptively concave, seeming to lean outward. So Ictinus designed columns that bulge slightly in the middle and taper near the top, while leaning slightly inward. The effect is unique, creating an apparently flawless geometry whose pure lines defy the gravity-bent, horizon-curved dictates of nature.

The centerpiece of the Acropolis is the Parthenon ("the Virgins' Place"), a temple in Doric style dedicated to the goddess Athena, the undefiled patron of the city. If Western civilization can be said to have a single birthplace, this is it. To stand on the Acropolis today is to gaze across not only the 25 miles that the view commands but also across the 25 centuries since Pericles and the Athenians sought—and decisively earned—eternal glory. ■

The Colosseum

Rome • A.D. 80
Architect unknown

The Colosseum in Rome was erected on the exact site of Nero's Golden House, where the Emperor supposedly fiddled as he watched his city burn, in a fire he may have ordered set in A.D. 64. This great building was not only baptized in bloodshed: it was built for bloodletting, for here gladiators fought to the death. Begun by Nero's successor Vespasian in A.D. 71, it was completed by his son Titus nine years later. The building is a triumph of design: its elliptical shape guarantees that every seat has good sight lines, while sturdy, rounded Roman arches support four mighty tiers, rising to 160 ft. (48 m), that seated some 50,000 spectators. (The half-columns flanking the arches are mainly for show, not support.) Below the 290-ft. by 180-ft. (88 m by 55 m) surface of the arena, a maze of corridors held chambers for gladiators, cages for animals and storage space for stage machinery. Trapdoors allowed direct access to the arena floor, making for stunning surprise entrances and ensuring speedy removal of the dead and wounded.

A prototype for today's giant sports arenas, the Colosseum is kin to the great outdoor amphitheaters of the Greeks and Spain's bull rings. In its heyday it was covered by an ingenious canvas awning that kept the sunshine and rain at bay. Its ruined state is not simply the work of time; it is the work of vandals—not barbarian tribes, but much later builders who plundered the structure for its limestone and marble. The process took centuries: after all, Rome wasn't unbuilt in a day. ∎

Grand Central Terminal

New York City • 1871 • Warren & Wetmore/Reed & Stem, architects

In the 1930s, listeners across America tuned in each Thursday night to the NBC Blue network, as an announcer breathlessly intoned, "Drawn by the magnetic force of the fantastic metropolis, day and night great trains rush toward … Grand Central Station! Crossroads of a million lives! Gigantic stage on which are played a thousand dramas daily." The show got the name wrong: it's Grand Central Terminal—not Station, despite what everybody says. But it got the sense of great doings exactly right. With its lofty barrel-vaulted concourse (275 ft. long, 120 ft. wide and 125 ft. high; 83 m by 36 m by 38 m), massive ceremonial staircases and swank public areas, Grand Central seems to enlarge the life of everyone who passes through it.

Wrecker's ball The demolition of New York City's soaring Pennsylvania Station, above, in 1964 to make way for a profoundly ordinary glass-and-steel office tower, in the basement of which a new train station was stuffed, was little more than vandalism. As the noted architectural historian Vincent Scully would later write, "One entered the city like a god … one scuttles in now like a rat."

The station was modeled on Rome's Baths of Caracalla: its main entrance was adorned with a two-block-long row of Doric columns, each 35 ft. high and 4 ft. in diameter (10 m by 1.2 m). Inside, the waiting room was the size of the nave of St. Peter's Basilica, with a vaulted ceiling 150 ft. (46 m) high. Completed in 1910, the station was one of the defining structures of its age and the signature piece of designers McKim, Mead & White, then the leading practitioners of classical design in America. But when the fortunes of the great railroads declined, the station's bankrupt owners quietly sold the edifice to developers, who tore it down and dumped the pieces in a New Jersey swamp. Public outrage led directly to the passage of the nation's first landmarks preservation law, which was quickly invoked to grant New York City's other great station, Grand Central Terminal, protected status.

A reluctant collaboration by two rival architectural firms, Warren & Wetmore and Reed & Stem, the structure is built on piers several levels above its submerged railroad tracks, whose placement underground made room for New York City's great boulevard, Park Avenue. The architects managed to make the building seem bigger inside than out by placing the floor of its concourse at the bottom of the ceremonial stairs at each entrance, submerging it below street level.

In the late 1960s the building was in deep decline and was almost demolished. Finally a $100 million refurbishing in the 1990s cleared World War II blackout paint from the terminal's windows, removed a huge billboard that blocked the sunlight and erased decades of grime from the ceilings, revealing a long-obscured mural of the night sky, complete with twinkling, lighted constellations. Redeemed, restored and resplendent, this space so central to the city is once again grand. ■

TWA Flight Center

New York City • 1962
Eero Saarinen, architect

Fresh from presiding over the 1957 design contest that awarded the commission for the Sydney Opera House to an unknown Jorn Utzon, Finnish architect Eero Saarinen remained captivated by the young Dane's idea for cladding the structure in a series of segmented shells. At the time, Saarinen was looking for a visual theme to breathe life into an upcoming project of his own: the new terminal for Trans World Airlines at New York City's Idlewild Airport (now John F. Kennedy International Airport). But where Utzon found inspiration for his masterpiece in the curve of an orange peel, Saarinen took his cue from a different source. As his associate, Kevin Roche, would later recall, "Eero was eating breakfast one morning and was using the rind of his grapefruit to describe the terminal shell. He pushed down its center to mimic the depression that he desired, and the grapefruit bulged."

From these convexities, Saarinen developed the idea for a soaring, arched roof that would trace the outline of a dome divided into four vaulting segments, each 50 ft. (15 m) high and 315 ft. (96 m) long. In his final design, each part of the dome touches the ground at only two points. But all four lobes converge at the navel of the terminal's roof (the point where Saarinen pressed down on his grapefruit, below) and lean against one another to form the third "leg" of support, balance and stability.

Admiring critics and the public swooned, seeing the building as an architectonic metaphor for flight: the eagle-like silhouette of its entrance portal boasted a beak and talons, while its soaring rooflines mimicked wings in flight. The architect, for whatever reasons, professed to be shocked by the notion. A good try, but no sale: Saarinen later admitted that "the shapes were deliberately chosen in order to emphasize an upward-soaring quality of line. We wanted an uplift."

When the building opened in 1962, a backlash against the International Style had been gathering momentum for years. For many, Saarinen's playful, curvilinear creation offered a beautiful alternative to the severe angularities of mainstream Modernism. His design also reflected the boundless optimism of the early 1960s, when companies like TWA built for the ages, sizing up trophy terminals the way Pharaohs eyed their pyramids. But if forward-looking in design, the building's smallish public areas looked backward to an era when air travel was for the privileged few, rather than the masses; it wore a tiara in an age of blue jeans.

Saarinen once reflected that the job of the architect was to place something "between earth and sky." With the TWA Flight Center, he succeeded so completely that both the ground below and the air above seem improved by his mediation. ■

Dynamic flow Inside, swooping curves convey a sense of fluid motion; a clock hangs where the vaults converge at the building's navel. In recent decades the debut of larger jets, the explosion of air travel into a mass-market commodity and heightened security measures left the original building overcrowded and undersized. Trans World Airlines struggled through several bankruptcies and was finally acquired by a competitor in 2001. The terminal building was saved in a 2003 agreement under which a new airline will use the space as a grand entrance foyer and ticketing center for a larger terminal; as of 2010, Saarinen's building remains under renovation for this purpose.

Burj al-Arab Hotel

Dubai, United Arab Emirates • 1999 • Tom Wright, architect

When the rulers of (then) oil-wealthy Dubai in the United Arab Emirates set out to turn their nation into a major tourist destination in the 1990s, they asked British architect Tom Wright to create an icon—a building like the Sydney Opera House or Eiffel Tower—that would bring worldwide attention to this land of only 700,000 people. Wright's Burj al-Arab (Arabian) Hotel rose to the challenge. Built on an artificial island, it recalls the shape of the sail-powered dhows that have long plied these waters.

The Burj al-Arab is one of the world's tallest hotels, at 1,050 ft. (321 m). But it's more than height that commands our attention: it's the building's bold engineering and its jaw-dropping bells and whistles, designed to provide envy-inducing talking points for the world's wealthiest travelers. Among them:

the lily-pad heliport at top, which connects directly to a lavish penthouse, and an underwater restaurant, accessible only by submarine.

The building is braced against strong sea winds by a three-part exoskeleton, with a pair of tuning-fork masts on one side and another curving mast at the rear that takes the shape of a taut bowstring. Inside, a lofty atrium runs the full height of the structure. The beautiful "sail" is more than a grace note: its Teflon-coated fiber-glass skin provides a screen from the withering sun, reducing heat and light in the interior, while it hides additional bracing. At night, the sail provides a backdrop for elaborate light shows—a reminder that Dubai is closer to Las Vegas than you might think. How much does it cost to spend the night here? If you have to ask, you probably won't be visiting. ■

Lyons Airport Railway Station

Lyons, France • 1994 • Santiago Calatrava, architect

Yes, it is extravagant. Yes it begs for the attention it receives. Yes, it "makes you look!" The railroad station at the Lyons Airport in France is one of the buildings dating to the 1990s with which the Spaniard Santiago Calatrava declared his intention of joining architecture's first rank of shapemakers. With its two mighty wings, the station is in part a homage to Finnish architect Eero Saarinen's birdlike TWA Flight Center at Kennedy International Airport in New York City; Calatrava often cites the Finn as a key influence. But as for why a train station should resemble an insect—the two front pillars that support the station's central "carapace" and side wings strongly suggest a proboscis—well, that's Calatrava's secret. Surely this was one of the buildings curator Matilda McQuaid of New York City's Museum of Modern Art had in mind when she wrote that Calatrava's work succeeds in "reaffirming a place for awe in the criteria for building."

Completed in 1994 at a cost of $200 million, the monumental station reflects its designer's intense interest in organic forms. Proud of his background in engineering, Calatrava once said, "Architects work in abstract terms, while engineers work more with models of nature." ■

Cooper Square

New York City • 2009
Thom Mayne, architect

The East Village is a New York City neighborhood with a complicated vibe, where restaurant equipment wholesalers and ancient brick walk-ups rub shoulders with spanking-new condo towers and hip hotels with signature martinis. For nearly 150 years one of the neighborhood's anchors has been the venerable main building of the Cooper Union for the Advancement of Science and Art, a college where presidents from Abraham Lincoln to Barack Obama have come to speak.

It's difficult to insert a new building into those streets and get it to speak to so many different contexts. The ideal combination of grit and elegance, muscle and intellect is hard to arrive at. But Cooper Union's new academic building, Cooper Square, which opened its doors in the fall of 2009, is a genuine triumph, a canny exercise in architectural multilingualism.

The building was designed by Morphosis, the Santa Monica–based firm of the Pritzker Prize–winning architect Thom Mayne, 65 in 2009. He makes buildings like no one else's, with complex orchestrations of space and form and a tough luster that's unmistakably his. The signature feature of Cooper Square's exterior is a perforated steel scrim that acts as both a sunscreen and an instant attention-grabber. By its folds and slashes it provides a dynamic surface to what might otherwise be a standard stack of offices, classrooms and laboratories, creating a concave façade that bows in many directions. Depending on the light, that steel skin, which has a low, semi-matte luster, can project either cheese-grater roughness or elegant shimmer—or, oddly, both. Sloping forward in its upper and lower portions, it gives the building's principal façade an elastic thrust that's both graceful and forceful. At street level, steel trusses appear from beneath the lower hem of the screen like sturdy legs beneath a swelling skirt.

The leaping gash that cuts through the Cooper Union façade is a gesture toward transparency; it corresponds to the public areas of the building and discloses them to the outside. Inside, Mayne has provided another bravura gesture, a stairway framed in places by a fluid, torquing gridwork

Grand canyon The building's main stairway serves as a gathering place. Most elevators do not stop at every floor, inviting people to take the stairs, encouraging bustle and unexpected encounters.

of white-painted steel that whirlpools upward through the building's multistory atrium, brimming with so much visual energy the stairs seem to be climbing themselves. But Mayne wants it to be understood as a resting place. "We talked about the space as a 'vertical piazza'," he told TIME. "It's an idea that goes back to the Renaissance or to the Spanish Steps, a stairway in which the main purpose isn't just movement up and down. It's a place used for gathering and sitting." And, he might have added, as a sort of scenic overlook for the building's spectacular interior landscapes. ∎

The Water Cube

Beijing • 2007
PTW Architects, architects

The building's formal name is the National Aquatics Center, but everyone calls it the Water Cube. Designed as a venue for the swimming events for the 2008 Beijing Olympic Games by the Australian firm PTW Architects, it made almost as big a splash as its neighbor, the Bird's Nest amphitheater at right. The bubbles on the building's exterior are not add-ons that evoke water: they *are* its exterior. They're composed of ethylene tetrafluoroethylene (ETFE), a transparent plastic polymer that admits more light than glass and is much sturdier and less expensive to install. The "cube" constitutes a technological break-through and signpost to the future as the largest ETFE-clad building in the world. The structure of the polymer envelopes was modeled on the geometry of soap bubbles, and the building is almost as evanescent: its interior has been gutted and it is being converted into an indoor shopping arcade and water park. ∎

The Sculptor of Spaces

Enlivening Modernism's straight lines with an artist's eye for nature, Santiago Calatrava creates a new poetry of design

Like his revolutionary buildings—which call to mind both the bleached bones of dinosaurs from the distant past and otherworldly edifices from the far-off future—Spanish architect Santiago Calatrava eludes labels. He is an architect above all, but he is also a trained engineer, an urban planner and a gifted artist who often finds inspiration for his designs in his watercolors and sculptures. All these skills seem to be on display in every building he designs: the mind is engaged as abstract principles of physics take concrete form, even as the senses are wooed by the sheer, arresting beauty of his shapes, which often suggest natural forms: wings, praying hands, a mastodon's rib cage, an eyeball.

Calatrava's work makes familiar formulations—like the eternal tension between form and function—seem instantly dated, obsolete. Like Frank Gehry, he creates buildings whose "wow" factor makes people fall in love with architecture's possibilities—though Gehry often wraps the bones of his buildings in shiny wrappers, whereas Calatrava loves to expose them. And although the architect's best work to date has been done in Europe, Americans are increasingly waking up to the fact that one of history's master designers is in his prime and bearing gifts: in the years to come, Chicago and New York City will join Milwaukee, Wis., in harboring major structures by Calatrava.

Born in 1951 near Valencia, Calatrava was fascinated by design early on; he claims he is still inspired by the soaring Gothic columns of a mercantile exchange he visited as a boy. He earned a degree in architecture in Valencia but put off practicing to study civil engineering, receiving his doctorate in 1979. He didn't begin working as a designer until he was 30, but he soon won a reputation as a bridge builder: he has designed almost 50 bridges in various European countries. Typical of his audacious way with a span is the Alamillo Bridge (1992) across the Guadalquivir River in the southern Spanish city of Seville. The 820-ft. roadway does not rest on piers; instead, it is suspended, held by cables stretching out from a single pylon, which leans back from the roadway at an angle of 58°—a hand grasping harp strings. Like much of Calatrava's work, the Alamillo Bridge can be traced to one of his sculptures, in this case a work he called *Running Torso,* a stack of marble cubes balanced by a taut wire.

From bridges, Calatrava soon graduated to transit stations: his train terminals in Lyons, France, and Lisbon manage to ennoble everyday commuting. His biggest project so far is for his native city: Valencia's $300 million City of Arts and Sciences is an enormous civic park that has reinvigorated the city's core with its planetarium, an eye-shaped hemisphere set in a huge pond, and its central Science Museum. From some angles, the museum's white concrete and cascades of glass conjure a dinosaur's spine caught in an ice floe. From others, they're a soaring forest of petrified trees.

Calatrava's debt to nature assumes even more palpable form when he treats his buildings as kinetic sculptures. A number of his bridges open up to allow ships to pass through them, while Valencia's eye-shaped planetarium sports a canopy that can be lowered like an eyelid. For a Roman Catholic cathedral proposed for Oakland (and now canceled) he designed a roof that opened and closed, suggesting two hands in prayer. His most prominent building in the U.S. to date also moves: the Milwaukee Art Museum entrance hall is topped with two giant "wings" that open up and flap in the wind, suggesting a gigantic bird or butterfly.

In January 2004, Calatrava showed off another kinetic building: a new transit hub to be built at ground zero in lower Manhattan. The terminal, featuring soaring 150-ft. white pylons and transparent glass walls, would be topped by a roof that would open with a hydraulic system to help cool it in the summer—and to allow a wedge of light to enter each year on Sept. 11. Funding woes have now trimmed the project's wings—one of the few times a Calatrava project has failed to soar. ∎

MITCH JENKINS

CITY OF ARTS AND SCIENCES, VALENCIA, 1998-2005

This huge project opened over a period of years. The planetarium, above, resembles an eyeball, complete with a canopy that opens and closes like an eyelid. Critics have assailed the playful aspects of Calatrava's designs as self-indulgent, but the architect delights in stimulating and entertaining those who use his buildings.

ALAMILLO BRIDGE, SEVILLE, SPAIN, 1992

By using a single pylon rather than two, Calatrava turned a simple span into a soaring essay in tension. The design, suggesting a lyre or harp, converts kinetic energy from abstract theory into physical fact. Filled with concrete, the steel-encased pylon rises 466 ft. (142 m) above the roadway.

"My approach to sculpture and architecture is always watching the behavior of the natural world." —SANTIAGO CALATRAVA

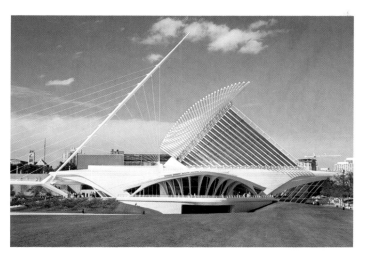

MILWAUKEE ART MUSEUM, 2003

Beam me up, Scotty! Calatrava's entrance building for Milwaukee's museum, left, has been hailed as a masterpiece and denounced as a gimmick. Its 72 steel white fins (beneath the prominent front mast), unfurl (on a strict schedule) from a cone shape to create a brise-soleil, or sunshade, whose two wings flap in the breeze.

The building's interior, below left, is equally futuristic. A successful flytrap for tourists, the entrance hall is all container and little content: it doesn't hold much art, following a recent trend in which museums commission trophy buildings that are destinations in themselves.

PROPOSED TRANSIT HUB, NEW YORK CITY

In January 2004, Calatrava unveiled his design for a new transit station that will arise at ground zero on the site of the former World Trade Center. Now modified, its transparent entrance hall will still bring natural light to platforms deep underground.

Petronas Towers, Malaysia *By the dawn's early light, window cleaners prepare to start their day atop one of the twin towers in Kuala Lumpur, at one time the world's tallest buildings*

Where We Work

Treasury at Petra

**Petra, Jordan • Circa 100 B.C. to A.D. 200
Architect unknown**

Deep in the desert, three hours by car from Amman, Jordan's capital city, stands all that remains of the great civilization of the Nabataeans—although stands may not be the right word for striking buildings hewed out of solid rock. We know the place by the name the Greeks gave it: Petra, Greek for stone. And certainly the Hellenic influence is present in the remarkable buildings at this site, of which the Treasury building, or al-Khazneh, at left, is the largest and most famous: its pediment and Corinthian columns are the unmistakable signature of the culture that built the Acropolis, although there are also Egyptian elements in the carvings on the façade. The name of the building is perhaps a misnomer; it may have been a royal tomb, perhaps holding a dead king's riches at one time.

Originally a nomadic Arab people, the Nabataeans settled in this region of wind- and water-carved canyons around the 6th century B.C. Through its mile-long main canyon, the Sik, passed caravans bearing pottery, silk and spices from Asia to Arabia and the Mediterranean. But the Nabataeans controlled the Sik, and they demanded tribute of all who ventured through.

Yet if the Nabataeans' wealth was ill-gotten, it was well spent. They mastered hydraulic technology, channeling water through tunnels carved into the hills and along elaborate ceramic pipes to irrigate the land. They also excelled at pottery and metallurgy. By 100 B.C. the Nabataeans commanded a mighty empire of trade with outposts around the Mediterranean, and Petra was a flourishing capital that boasted an 8,000-seat theater, temples, proud villas and broad avenues, the remains of which can still be seen. Petra's wealth attracted the interest of the Romans, who became the first to conquer the city: the Emperor Trajan entered it in A.D. 106. The city continued to flourish under Roman rule, until an earthquake destroyed many of its buildings in A.D. 363; two centuries later, another earthquake led inhabitants to leave the city forever. Thinly resettled in recent centuries, Petra was "lost" to Europeans until Swiss explorer Johann Burkhardt, disguised as a Muslim, managed to enter the city in 1812. ∎

Galeria Vittorio Emanuele

Milan • 1867
Giuseppi Mengoni, architect

I f shopping malls aren't envious of skyscrapers, they should be. From humble beginnings, the skyscraper has grown steadily taller, more daring, more fascinating. But its contemporary, the shopping mall, has traced precisely the opposite trajectory: it's all been downhill since architect Giuseppi Mengoni brilliantly reimagined urban space with the Galeria Vittorio Emanuele, which opened in Milan in 1867.

To see the *Ur*-mall—the lofty prototype your local box of franchise joints utterly fails to live up to—take a stroll past Milan's great cathedral on your way to the legendary opera house, La Scala, and turn into the Galeria. Your heart will soar as your gaze travels upward ... and upward ... to meet the glass vault 120 ft. (36 m) above that shelters you from the elements, as it casts a dim diurnal glow on the façades around you. While Mengoni's Galeria is not the first enclosed pedestrian shopping mall in Europe—London, Paris and Brussels had smaller antecedents— this great space was seen as revolutionary when it opened in 1867, and, in forbidding automobiles, it remains one of the earth's most user-friendly urban environments.

The first iron-and-glass gallery built in Europe, the Galeria looks backward to the landmark 1851 Crystal Palace in London and forward to a host of great train stations. It is charged with the fresh energy of its time, when Italy's long-squabbling republics began to unite and a new dawn for the nation was at hand. Sadly, the architect did not live to see that dawn: two days before the Galeria opened, he slipped and fell to his death from atop one of the buildings under his vault. ■

Out on a limb Walter Chrysler hired Margaret Bourke-White, a 23-year-old whose pictures of factories had made a splash in Henry Luce's new business magazine, FORTUNE, to photograph his prized building. "Art that springs from industry should have real flesh and blood, because industry itself is the vital force of this great age," she once wrote, in what sounds like an Art Deco manifesto. At left, she perches on one of the giant steel-coated eagle gargoyles located where the primary tower begins narrowing to meet the spire.

Chrysler Building

New York City · 1930
William van Alen, architect

Like the soaring Gothic cathedrals of the Middle Ages, skyscrapers are exercises in aspiration and uplift, optimism frozen in girders and glass. No building better captures the pure exhilaration of the form than the needle-nosed number William van Alen designed for auto magnate Walter Chrysler in 1930. It's the Buck Rogers top that we can't get enough of: a cascade of Art Deco arches urged upward by giant, spiky triangular windows, it seems to be perpetually unfolding, organic and alive. The rest of the building is just as daring, for Van Alen, who had studied in Paris as a winner of a scholarship sponsored by the American Society of Beaux Arts Architects, adorned it with a hodgepodge of automotive-age details that somehow work: giant eagle gargoyles (modeled on Chrysler hood ornaments); a frieze of oversized hubcaps; abstract images of motorcars. The lobby murals feature airplanes and Detroit assembly lines—Art Deco's love affair with machines. Alive with the feel of its time, Van Alen's work exposes such Gothic Revival towers as Manhattan's Woolworth Building (1913) and Chicago's Tribune Tower (1925) as stylistic dead ends.

Sadly, Walter Chrysler's interest in the building centered on its short-lived title as the world's tallest; once it was overpowered by its crosstown rival, the Empire State Building, he quarreled with Van Alen, refused to pay his fee and ended up litigating with him. And that's too bad, because in this great structure Chrysler scrawled his name indelibly on Manhattan's skyline. "The age demanded an image/ Of its accelerated grimace," Ezra Pound wrote about the irrational exuberance of the early 20th century. Van Alen's dynamic Chrysler Building makes the velocity vertical and turns the grimace into a grin. ∎

Empire State Building

New York City • 1931
William Lamb, architect

Conceived in competition, baptized in ballyhoo and calibrated for comparison, the Empire State Building is dedicated to the proposition that all skyscrapers are not created equal. This most emblematic of urban structures was the winner of a frantic race to the sky, as New York City developers and architects vied to capture the title of world's tallest building. The contest was a final frantic spasm of jazz-age optimism before the stock-market crash of 1929—but so strong was the impetus behind the Empire State Building (and so deep were the pockets of its builders) that riveters kept joining its girders even as sightings of scaffolding grew scarce in Manhattan's streets. The long years of economic woe and the great labors of World War II ensured that no rival would top its 1,250-ft. (381 m) height for decades. The Twin Towers of the World Trade Center finally stole the building's thunder in 1971, and Chicago's Sears Tower soon topped them. More behemoths have followed. No matter. When we think of skyscrapers, this is it—the icon.

Fueled by new media, including radio, newsreel films and mass magazines like TIME, the 1920s were a Barnumesque era of publicity stunts, gaudy spectacles and giddy excess. In the world of business and real estate, the age's Olympian impulses—swifter, higher, stronger—saw tycoons trying to top one another by constructing ever taller edifices. In Manhattan, the year 1928 saw two moguls, automaker Walter Chrysler, TIME's Man of the Year, and Wall Street wunderkind George Ohrstrom, a multimillionaire at only 33, locked in a battle to erect the world's tallest building. As Neal Bascomb tells the story in his engaging account *Higher* (Doubleday; 2003), Chrysler and architect William van Alen won the contest by waiting until their building was almost completed, then erecting its spire by surprise. But their glee was short-lived, for both Ohrstrom's 40 Wall Street and the Chrysler Building were soon dwarfed by a late entry, the Empire State Building.

Designed by architect William Lamb, it was the brainchild of Chrysler's rival John J. Raskob, a top General Motors executive.

Completed in 1931, the building has spawned legends. Hollywood immortalized it as a jungle-gym for the giant ape King Kong in the classic 1933 movie. On July 28, 1945, 13 people died after a B-25 bomber pilot, lost in fog, rammed his plane into the building's 78th floor. In 1961 control of the building was acquired by real estate maven Harry Helmsley; in the next decade, he and his imperious wife and partner Leona illuminated its top with colored lights at night; the hues change to celebrate holidays, seasons, visitors to the city, even winning sports teams. Kitschy? Yes—but somehow the colors seem a fitting crown for this monarch of buildings.

On the morning of Sept. 11, 2001, workers on the upper floors of the structure were startled to hear a passenger jet roaring downtown along the Hudson River at low altitude and top speed: hours later, the Empire State Building was once again the tallest skyscraper in Manhattan. This time around, it was a distinction smothered in sorrow. ∎

Twin Towers, World Trade Center

New York City • 1971
Minoru Yamasaki, architect

They became the world's tallest twins by accident. When the Port Authority of New York and New Jersey set out to build the World Trade Center in the late 1960s, plans called for 10 million sq. ft. of office space, which could have been spread across the 16-acre site in lower Manhattan in any number of ways. But after a public relations person blithely suggested that the project might be designed to create the loftiest skyscraper in the world, the "biggest" bug took hold. One tower became two when architect Minoru Yamasaki decided that a pair of slender columns thrusting skyward would be less oppressive than a single, stout massif.

Yamasaki, an advocate of "a friendly, more gentle kind of building," had made his reputation with office towers that wove strands of concrete and steel into complex, delicate surfaces that looked very much like textiles. And the Twin Towers would be no exception: their narrow columns and vertical stripes of glass, set back in shadow, would give them the appearance of being clad in pinstripes. Inspired by sources as diverse as the Doge's Palace in Venice (its romantic motif of arches culminating in columns shaped the towers' ground floors) and the Katsura Imperial Villa in Kyoto (whose slender bamboo fence was echoed in the slim vertical lines that reached a quarter-mile into the clouds), Yamasaki labored mightily to create giants that were still human in scale. But when they were finally completed in 1971, the minimalist style and maximalist size of the big twins made them hard to love—and the failure to incorporate the towers and their plaza into the street grid of lower Manhattan made them seem isolated, overbearing intruders rather than friendly neighbors. Even the "world's tallest" bragging rights were fleeting: in 1974 Chicago's Sears Tower surpassed the twins in height by less than 100 ft. (30 m).

New Yorkers initially groused that the spare behemoths looked like the boxes that the beloved Empire State Building and Chrysler Building came wrapped in. But just as the Eiffel Tower grew on Parisians who initially hated it, New Yorkers came to take a grudging pride in the silvery tuning fork that anchored their skyline. The towers were at their best in the evening: transformed into pillars of light, they rose as icons of optimism and power, fitting companions to America's nearby beacon of freedom, the Statue of Liberty. As the song says, "Don't it always seem to go/ That you don't know what you've got till it's gone?" ∎

HSBC Building

Hong Kong • 1986
Norman Foster, architect

At first glance, the buildings of former partners Norman Foster and Richard Rogers seem to be all about their surfaces: their inside-out, high-tech designs transform boring infrastructures into witty façades. But beyond exulting in innards, their designs reflect deep thinking about the way buildings work and the way people work within them. When Foster won a 1979 contest to design the headquarters of the Hong Kong & Shanghai Banking Corp. (HSBC) in Hong Kong, he reimagined the skyscraper from the ground up: how it supports itself; how light enters the building; how workers move around within it; even what they see, for he managed to turn every office into a room with a view. (Foster's building is at right; the striking skyscraper at left rear is the Bank of China Tower, designed by I.M. Pei.)

Foster sought to open up the building, so it wouldn't be a confining stack of vertical boxes. Rather than support his floors by channeling their weight downward, he hung modular office blocks from giant, inverted V-shaped trusses, visible on the façade. The trusses, in turn, are supported by enormous masts at the ends of the building, much as a roadway hangs from the pylons of a suspension bridge. Service elements such as elevators and heating ducts are housed in the end masts. In most office buildings, valuable space at the center of each floor is set aside for these core functions, but this unique design leaves the interiors of the floors wide open, creating a sense of enormous spaciousness.

To divide the 47-story building into "villages," its elevators stop only every five floors. To move between nearby floors, workers ride one of 162 escalators, completely visible and humming with movement: this place is a beehive of activity. On the lower floors a 10-story atrium makes a grandly imposing entry hall; its ground-floor plaza is a lively gathering place for locals. On the roof, the mirrors of Foster's trademark "sunscoops" funnel natural sunlight throughout the building, illuminating not only the interior of this building but also a way forward for office towers of the future. ∎

Big story An extensive mall sits between the towers, offering a large space for retail and entertainment use, including a theater, a petroleum exhibit (Petronas is the national oil company of Malaysia) and a parking facility. The diameter of each slim tower's central core is only 150 ft. (45 m), while the circular design maximizes window space. Atop one tower, the Billionaire's Club restaurant, above, swoops in an elegant swirl.

Petronas Towers

Kuala Lumpur, Malaysia • 1997
César Pelli, architect

When it comes to skyscrapers, size matters: the more flights, the more bragging rights. Since their first appearance in Chicago in the 1870s, the big spires have flourished on the generous fertilizer spread by glory-seeking architects, tycoons with edifice complexes and civic boosters frantic to top the next town's tower, if only by a smidgen. This recipe created America's big skyscrapers, and it's the force that has more recently powered towers in Southeast Asia, China and the Middle East. Case in point: the Petronas Towers in Kuala Lumpur, Malaysia. In the unlikely event that they should ever find themselves adjacent to the building whose crown as tallest they stole in 1997, Chicago's Sears Tower (now Willis Tower), the two

1,476-ft. (450 m) spires would loom over the former champ by a commanding … 22 ft. (6.7 m). 'Nuf said?

Designed by Argentine-American architect César Pelli, the matching monsters reach 88 stories, are capped by 246-ft. (75 m) tapered pinnacles in classic Malaysian style and are connected by a skybridge. But alas, Petronas Towers: your elevator shafts may be long, but your reign was short. In 2004, Taipei 101, a 1,667-ft. (508 m) behemoth in Taiwan's capital snatched the title of world's tallest tower. And in 2010 it passed again, this time to the lofty Burj Khalifa in Dubai. If an institution is the lengthened shadow of one man, skyscrapers are the lengthened shadow of their builders' egos. And when it comes to builders' egos, size matters. ■

Gherkin Building

London • 2004
Norman Foster, architect

Y ou could say that Norman Foster's skyscraper at 30 St. Mary Axe street in the heart of the City of London, the British capital's historic financial center, is poised like a bullet against the skyline. But even before it was completed in 2004, Londoners seized upon a more playful moniker for the cartridge-shaped edifice: the Gherkin Building. And it's hard to deny that there's a certain gleeful relish in Foster's graceful, 590-ft. (180 m) structure.

As Katherine Tanko reported from TIME's London bureau, the tapering cylinder quickly became "a hit with everyone, from architects to heritage lovers to ordinary Londoners" soon after it was completed, with many hailing its environmentally smart design, which takes advantage of natural light and ventilation to use just half the energy of a typical office block. "The building's elegant outline," wrote Tanko, "has reassured locals that architecture can be both attractive and high-rise, even in a city that, as late as the 1960s, prohibited the construction of buildings taller than St. Paul's Cathedral."

The building also quickly became the capital's most exclusive events venue. Its top two floors house a glass-domed private restaurant that is hired out for functions. Sadly, plans that called for additional big skyscrapers that promised to further move the City of London into the future were sidetracked by the worldwide recession that began in 2008. Among those now on hold is a mammoth, semitransparent wedge-shaped building designed by British architect Richard Rogers that design-hungry Londoners had already dubbed "the Cheesegrater." ∎

Burj Khalifa

Dubai, United Arab Emirates • 2010
Adrian D. Smith, architect

The skyscraper was born in the U.S., and for most of the 20th century, the form flourished here. As of 1989, nine of the world's 10 tallest buildings were in the U.S. (The 10th was in Toronto.) Now none are. A mix of factors—a sluggish commercial real estate market, skepticism about the profitability of very tall buildings even in good times, the rise of urban thinking critical of skyscrapers and the psychological fallout from 9/11—has discouraged today's American developers from going very, very high.

More subtly, for some time before 9/11, the tall building had been losing ground as a symbol of power, wealth and importance in Western countries, where museums, shops and restaurants became more significant status indicators. But elsewhere in the world, extreme verticals are still entirely in fashion, especially for developing nations seeking to announce themselves. Looking for tall buildings? Follow the money.

In the first years of the new century, that trail led to the vibrant economies of the Pacific Rim. Asia became the last outpost of post-Modernism, the ornamental style that American architects tried for a while in the 1980s, struggling to link the office tower to older traditions of Western building by tarting it up with Gothic spires and classical pediments. Post-modernism was an awkward undertaking, and it fell out of fashion in the U.S. when architects began finding more interesting frontiers beyond the stylistic endgame of Modernism.

Not in Asia, however. Many Asian clients saw the plain glass-and-steel Modernist box as a Western import, remote from their national traditions. They wanted silhouettes that would recollect local styles. So the Petronas Towers in Malaysia, at one time the tallest buildings in the world, evoke the minarets of a mosque expanded to sky-high proportions. The Jin Mao Tower in Shanghai is a highly elongated pagoda.

So is Taiwan's Taipei 101, a giant knickknack of a building that pushes the post-Modernist idea to the edge of kitsch—or past it.

But no nation in the world embraced the taller-is-better aesthetic more fully than Dubai, a center of Middle East finance and one of the seven small states of the United Arab Emirates. On Jan. 4, 2010, the Burj Khalifa in Dubai opened its doors as the world's tallest building, blowing past all competitors at the stunning height of 2,625 ft. (800 m)—not even counting its slender spire. Do the math: the building, which boasts more than 160 stories, ascends more than half a mile into the sky. It was designed by the well-known architect Adrian D. Smith, formerly of the Chicago office of Skidmore Owings & Merrill, the firm that has been in the forefront of skyscraper design since the mid-20th century.

Composed of three lobes that form a Y shape on its lower floors, the building resembles the bundled-tube form of Chicago's Willis (formerly Sears) Tower and other recent skyscrapers. But it narrows to a single column as it rises, echoing the classic "needle in the sky" look of many classic 20th century skyscrapers.

Rare for a building so large, the structure has more residential condominiums than offices; like Dubai itself, it hopes to serve as a safe harbor for investment capital for the world's wealthiest citizens and companies. It also is home to an upscale hotel operated by Giorgio Armani. But when Dubai's high-flying economy collapsed in 2008-09, construction slowed on the giant building, which was to be named the Burj Dubai (Dubai Tower). Dubai's more secure neighbor, oil-rich Abu Dhabi, came to the rescue, shoring up the project with $25 billions in loans. The skyscraper was quickly named the Burj Khalifa in honor of Abu Dhabi's ruler, Khalifa bin Zayed Al Nahyan. In this race to the top, nomenclature also followed the money. ∎

Master of the Modern

Ludwig Mies van der Rohe refined his buildings to their essentials, finding God in the details and poetry in geometry

Once lauded as the parent and patron saint of Modernist architecture, he would later be damned as the man who turned the world's cityscapes into drafty canyons lined by banal boxes of glass and steel. In truth, Ludwig Mies van der Rohe was neither angel nor devil. Rather, he was a stonemason's son from rural Germany who never lost his love for purity in materials, strength in expression and clarity in design.

Born in Aachen in 1886, Mies apprenticed to the influential German designer Peter Behrens. Influenced by religious thinkers like Augustine and Aquinas who emphasized intellectual rigor, he became obsessed with stripping away the ornamentation ("macaroni" he called it) he found in most European architecture. He was not above personal artifice, however; he added his mother's maiden name, Van der Rohe, to his own surname, which is German slang for "lousy."

Reluctantly designing neo-Georgian houses for clients as late as 1924, Mies first gained worldwide attention for his "honest" architecture with his German Pavilion at the Barcelona Exhibition in 1928. In this cool, confident temple, slender chrome-plated columns supported a thin, hovering roof slab and surrounded an open-plan interior divided by movable glass panels. The building converted an entire generation of young architects to Mies' clear-eyed vision of the future; sadly, it was demolished at the exhibition's end.

Mies' career almost followed suit. After Adolf Hitler took power in 1933, the reductive classicism favored by the Nazis became Germany's official style, a point underscored when the Nazis shut down the famed Bauhaus design school, where Mies had succeeded Walter Gropius as director. Encouraged by American acolytes of his emerging "International Style," Mies emigrated to the U.S. in 1938. Nine years later, when young architect Philip Johnson organized a show of the German's work at New York's Museum of Modern Art,

Mies was all but officially anointed the high priest of contemporary architecture. A series of massive masterpieces followed: the campus of the Illinois Institute of Technology, twin apartment towers on Chicago's Lake Shore Drive (right) and, most memorably, the Seagram Building in New York City. Each featured what Mies called "universal space" interiors: vast, vertical open-plan expanses that could serve any purpose, anywhere in the world. In each of them, structure became ornament: Mies exposed supporting girders that traditional architects had always hidden. By distilling buildings to their essential elements—vertical and horizontal planes, bare but lustrous materials—Mies created a rigorous new poetry of form. "God is in the details," he said.

The bronze-and-glass Seagram Building (1958), Mies' masterpiece, secured his position as the foremost form-giver of 20th century architects. Raised above street level on a block-long pink-granite platform, the elegant tower is set back on the site and framed by a broad plaza with reflecting pools. When first built, its luminous façade glowed against the masonry-clad buildings around it like a messenger from the future.

Yet the Seagram Building also contained the seeds of a backlash against Mies and Modernism. Just as many writers have found the lean prose of Ernest Hemingway easy to imitate but impossible to duplicate, lesser architects began aping Mies' spare, geometric style while missing his numinous details. Developers urged them on, for a skyscraper devoid of embellishment is a thing of beauty when viewed from the bottom line. The result was a generation of boring boxes that made Modernism a synonym for the banal.

Since Mies' death in 1961, the works of the master have increasingly stood out from those of his imitators. The austere German's reputation has risen from the ashes, and it isn't alone: in 1987, his great lost masterpiece, the German Pavilion for the Barcelona Exhibition, was rebuilt on its original site. ∎

NATIONAL GALLERY, BERLIN, 1968
The skillful use of glass gives Mies' buildings transparency and clarity. In the daytime, glass brings outdoor elements into the interiors of his buildings; in the nighttime, the illuminated structures become containers of light, glowing with beauty. Here, the main galleries are underground, below the terrace; temporary exhibits are housed within the glass-walled pavilion.

CHAPEL, ILLINOIS INSTITUTE OF TECHNOLOGY, CHICAGO, 1953
The sanctuary becomes a jewel box of light in this deceptively simple chapel, which blooms when the interior is illuminated. Mies designed 10 buildings at the Chicago technical university, extending the Windy City's reputation as a cradle for innovative architecture, which it first earned in the late 1800s.

"Less is more." —LUDWIG MIES VAN DER ROHE

TUGENDHAT HOUSE, CZECH REPUBLIC, 1930
Today, this interior looks almost generic: it could be the dining room of any modern home—and that's a tribute to the pervasive influence of Mies' stripped-down aesthetic. When the Tugendhat House was first built, its spare look was utterly revolutionary. It took years to perfect the resilient stainless steel that supports the innovative, iconic chairs designed by Mies.

GERMAN PAVILION, BARCELONA EXPOSITION, 1928
The walls disappear in Mies' groundbreaking building, obliterating the distinction between inside and out. Mies used the finest materials; imitators copied his geometry, minus the richness of detail.

SEAGRAM BUILDING, 1958
The building's front plaza is unfinished in this picture, which shows the key features of the design: exposed structural elements, glass façade, a transparent first floor over which the main edifice seems to float. When safety codes mandated that the building's structural steel girders be encased in concrete, Mies designed a second set of steel members to hang outside them, thus "revealing" the structural forms within. The architect's love of order sometimes gave way to a mania for control: he lost the battle to control every window shade in the building from a single master switch.

Piazza del Campidoglio, Rome
Two older buildings were given a facelift and a graceful third was added to form this plaza on a commanding hilltop overlooking Rome. The project was designed by Michelangelo, but it was not completed until long after the Italian master's death in 1564

Where Power Resides

Pyramid of the Magician

**Uxmal, Mexico • Circa 7th-11th centuries
Architects unknown**

At the center of Uxmal, the most exotic of the ancient cities in the Yucatán region of Mexico, the Pyramid of the Magician, el Adivino, rises into the sky. Unique among Maya pyramids, the design features an oval base and no right angles other than those found on the stairs and in the temple at its summit, which towers 117 ft. (35.5 m) above its surroundings. A path of 121 steps, each just 6 in. (15 cm) wide, ascends at a steep 60° angle to the temple.

The Maya kept complex and accurate celestial calendars: the pyramid is perfectly aligned to face the setting sun on the date of the summer solstice, while nearby buildings point to positions in the sky (on key dates) of all the planets known to the Maya. On a ball court, a sacred game was played: the leader of the winning team would often be honored by ascending to the top of the pyramid to have his heart torn out with a piece of flint. Human sacrifice was central to the Maya religion; some victims were decapitated, and their heads rolled down the stairs.

In the Maya language, *uxmal* means "thrice built"; the Maya often erected new structures on top of old ones. The pyramid may be the third version of the sacred structure, and there is evidence of five separate building periods in the city itself. Maya legend holds that the pyramid was built in a single night by a dwarf magician who had been hatched from an egg by his witch mother. A more likely candidate is Uxmal's greatest King, Chan Chak K'ak'nal Ahaw, who ruled the city around A.D. 800 and erected many temples and palaces.

Historians can't explain why Uxmal and other nearby Maya cities went into sudden decline after A.D. 1200. The leading theory is that the two deities honored in the Pyramid of the Magician, Itzamna (god of the sky) and Chac (god of rain), may have abandoned the Maya to a severe drought that strangled their culture. ∎

STEVE MCCURRY—MAGNUM PHOTOS

Palace of the Alhambra

Granada, Spain · 13th to 14th centuries
Architects unknown

Nestled among the tallest mountains in Spain, just outside Granada, is an exquisite palace-cum-fortress that represents the high-water mark of Islamic architectural achievement in Western Europe. The Alhambra (Arabic for "Red Castle," a nod to the tint of the clay in its bricks) was built by a succession of Moorish rulers in the Nasrid dynasty, beginning with Muhammad I in the 13th century. Their architects created a wholly original form, now known as caliphal style, that expresses the standard Moorish repertoire of arches, columns and domes in a new, intricately refined way that remains unique in the Islamic world. The numerous towers, courtyards and lavishly decorated interior rooms of the complex flow gracefully, almost fluidly into one another, creating an organic whole in which the wood and stone almost seem to breathe.

Within these walls, temporal power is not flaunted; rather, spiritual power is evoked, even wooed. Nowhere is this truer than in the interior courtyards, which feature serene rows of slender columns, gently burbling fountains and reflecting pools that induce a sense of otherworldly calm. The greatest of these, the Court of Lions, with its graceful arcades set atop 124 white marble columns, flouts the Koran's prohibition of figurative imagery (there are numerous reliefs of animals and plants) to create a vision of paradise as limned by Arab poets. To Muslims, this palace is more than just a place of beauty and a piece of history: it is a physical manifestation of Allah's presence in this world. In 1492, when Boabdil, the last Nasrid king, relinquished Granada to the armies of Catholic Spain, legend has it that he turned to gaze at his enchanted citadel one last time, then fell to his knees and wept. ■

Inner visions Inside the Alhambra, graphic and written references to the next world abound. The Alhambra's builders viewed empty wall space as a canvas crying out for artistic attention: graceful geometric patterns, endlessly repeated, and delicately carved calligraphy of Islamic poetry and verses from the Koran cover almost every square inch of surface on the walls and ceilings. Small windows foster a dappled interplay of light and shadow, while still pools in hushed courtyards reflect nature's majesty.

Tower of London

London • 11th to 12th centuries • Architects unknown

I f William the Conqueror, who began erecting the Tower of London in 1066, had been able to see all that would transpire there over the next 900 years, he might have packed up and returned to France. His London keep has variously served as a royal residence, a records warehouse, a zoo, a prison, a place of execution for two English Queens (and the site of the secret murders of one King, one duke and two princes), a royal mint, a home to the crown jewels and, most recently, a magnet for itinerary-dazed, camera-toting tourists.

As it was, the Norman ruler needed an impressive (and impregnable) fortification to clinch his strategic choke hold over London. Within months of taking power, he began work on a modest stone enclosure along the banks of the Thames, within a corner of the old Roman city walls. A few years later, he completed

the first version of his massive White Tower, above rear, a lofty medieval skyscraper fashioned by Norman masons from French stone. At 118 ft. (36 m), the square tower dominated London physically and its residents psychologically. In the centuries that followed, the site expanded into a vast complex that included moats, fortified walls, additional towers like the one in the foreground above, and a palace. In its first 600 years, the tower never quite shook off its first purpose, as a redoubt to which English royals could retreat in times of unrest. Nearly every British King, from William to the doomed Charles I, would take refuge in the tower during his reign. William the Conqueror used the words "vast and fierce" to describe the London populace his tower kept out—but the phrase perhaps better suits the fortress itself. ■

Himeji Castle

Osaka, Japan • 1601-10 • Architects unknown

On a hill overlooking a verdant Japanese plain 25 miles (40 km) west of bustling Osaka stands one of the most peaceful-looking, soaring fortresses in the world. Himeji Castle, named for the city it towers over, is also known as Shirasagijo ("White Heron Castle"), because its graceful, undulating lines recall the profile of the long-stemmed shorebird.

Replacing a 14th-century predecessor, the current structure was built in nine years by 50,000 pairs of hands and served as a regional stronghold for the Tokugawa shogunate. One of the few and best-preserved examples of Japanese 17th century fortress architecture extant, Himeji demonstrates that the nation's medieval architects couldn't stop themselves from creating beautiful, elegant structures—even when the build-ing's purpose was grimly utilitarian. Vertical slits in the castle's façade appear intended to allow a summer breeze to circulate within, but their real purpose was to permit archers to shoot at enemy soldiers below. Elegant spouts at the corners of the castle's successive rooftops look like sculpted rain gutters but were shaped to assist in pouring boiling oil onto besieging troops. A serpentine maze of sunken walkways (the only way to approach the base of the castle) seems designed to channel visitors past beautiful gardens but was actually intended to slow invaders, making them vulnerable to attack from above. Surrounded by three concentric moats and soaring 150 ft. (45 m) into the air, Himeji presented so daunting an obstacle to its enemies that this serene structure of war never saw a single battle. ∎

MIKE YAMASHITA

Château de Versailles

Outside Paris • 17th century
Jules Hardouin-Mansart, primary architect

Château de Versailles is both exhilarating and appalling: a symbol of France's cultural greatness, it is also a monument to political oppression. But dig deep enough, and it's a weekend cabin on steroids. The palace, which reached an apogee of excess in the decades preceding the French Revolution, began as a simple hunting lodge. Here, in the countryside some 20 miles (32 km) outside the Paris of his day, King Louis XIII would retreat from the burdens of court life to enjoy the hunt. In 1624 he built a modest lodge on the spot, and from that seed this most lavish of royal palaces grew ... and grew ... and grew. In 1631, Louis XIII added an eight-room château to the site. His son and heir, Louis XIV, was the true visionary of Versailles. The "Sun King" added on to the château three times and lavished attention on its extensive formal gardens, which were designed by master landscape architect André le Nôtre. By 1682, Louis XIV was so smitten with his creation (and its safe remove from urban strife) that he moved his entire court to Versailles: the onetime retreat from power's burdens was now power's epicenter.

Here three Louises—XIV, XV and XVI—conducted business and pleasure amid formalized courtly rituals that turned everyday life into royal performance art: hundreds of standing courtiers would gather in the queen's antechamber simply to watch the royal family dine. The increasingly elaborate palace and gardens were justified as representing the splendor of the nation, and in truth, diplomats and other visitors who cast wondering eyes upon the place must have left marveling at the riches of the French realm.

Built to impress, this royal residence is all about its inventory. So here goes: at its height, some 1,000 French nobles lived at Versailles, attended to by 6,000 servants. The longest wing of its edifice stretches for a quarter-mile; there were 200 pieces of solid-silver furniture, including the Sun King's 8-ft. (2.5 m) throne. By one estimate, half of France's annual revenue went to keeping up Versailles—until the bill came due in 1789. ■

Royal retreat Louis XIV, the "Sun King," is the presiding spirit of Versailles. Although he technically ascended to the throne of France in 1643 at age 4, he truly took power after the death of his regent, Cardinal Mazarin, in 1661. In the remaining 54 years of his reign, Louis became the most absolute of monarchs, and he shrewdly used the Château de Versailles as a symbol and tool of his power. He officially moved his royal residence from the Louvre in Paris to Versailles in 1682, far from the struggling masses in the city, whose 1648-53 uprising, termed La Fronde, had deeply worried the young King.

The exterior of the château is a bit dull; it is the interiors and extensive gardens, far right, that make this one of earth's most memorable places. The lavish Hall of Mirrors, near right, reflects a society in which appearances were paramount.

U.S. Capitol

Washington, D.C. • 1793-1863
William Thornton and
Benjamin Latrobe, architects

Standing in the swampy Maryland wilderness that was to become the District of Columbia, Pierre Charles L'Enfant scouted a promontory known in the 1790s as Jenkins Hill, which he described as "a pedestal waiting for a monument." The monument he planned to erect there, the U.S. Capitol Building, was, L'Enfant repeatedly claimed, already designed. Asked to produce the drawings, he demurred, saying they were stored "in his head." After the newborn Federal Government dismissed the irascible Frenchman, a design competition that promised $500 and one city lot to the winner settled on the neoclassical plan drawn up by William Thornton, a Scottish physician, painter and engineer living in the British West Indies who dabbled in architecture in his spare time.

Thornton's Palladian design for two rectangular wings connected by a central dome drew praise from George Washington for its "grandeur, simplicity and convenience." Reflecting the views of Washington's Federalist Party, the design allocated vast ceremonial space beneath a huge dome to palatial offices for a kinglike President. But after Washington's death in 1799, the more populist ideals of Thomas Jefferson and his followers took hold. Under a new architect, Benjamin Latrobe, the Rotunda of the building became, in Jefferson's words, "a hall of the people." The mammoth structure, whose dome stands 288 ft. (88 m) high, shelters 16 acres and more than 500 rooms. It has often been modified: a new underground entrance for visitors opened in 2008. Like the country it stands for, it is always a work in progress. ■

GEORGES DEKEERLE—GETTY IMAGES

Palace of Westminster

London • 1840-70
Charles Barry, architect

Properly perpendicular, proudly pinnacled and pickled in pomp, the Palace of Westminster, home of Britain's Parliament, indelibly embodies the culture of its people. Here, amid ornate walls and lofty spires, stained-glass windows and a royal Robing Room, in the shadow of centuries-old Big Ben, a visitor feels immersed in the great saga of British history. Turning a corner, one might expect to bump into

Disraeli, Gladstone or Churchill. But the most remarkable aspect of this ancient structure ... is that it isn't ancient. Nor is Big Ben "centuries old"—it dates to 1858.

When the venerable House of Parliament building, situated on the same enviable site, burned to the ground in 1834, it offered Britons a chance to erect a new home for the House of Commons and House of Lords that reflected the nation's history. The commit-

tee charged with choosing an architect decreed that the building must not be designed along Greek or Roman lines—British M.P.s should not convene behind the columns or beneath the dome of a "pagan" structure. The winning design, in a Gothic Revival style whose strong perpendicular elements were drawn from British cathedrals, was the work of Charles Barry.

The eccentric Augustus Pugin, an advocate and master of the Victorian Gothic style, labored for years on the building's interior details, sketching everything from floor tiles and coal buckets to doorknobs and inkstands. The building now bears history's scars: the House of Commons was destroyed by German bombs in 1941. At Prime Minister Winston Churchill's urging, its main hall was rebuilt at too small a size to seat all its members at once, in order to retain its intimate feel. ■

Cathedral

Congress Building

Foreign Ministry

Brasília

Federal District, Brazil • 1956-60
Oscar Niemeyer, architect

If the future that Modernism promised—but never quite delivered—has an address, it's a dusty savanna in the Brazilian state of Goiás, more than 500 miles from the nation's cultural center, Rio de Janeiro. Brazil's President, Juscelino Kubitschek, decided in 1955 to relocate the country's capital city to this uninhabited wasteland, a tabula rasa upon which his nation could sketch its future with a free hand. A wondrous tomorrow for Brazil was just around the corner, he seemed to believe, if he could just build the right structures to house it.

The noted Swiss-French prophet of Modernism Le Corbusier dreamed of demolishing Paris and replacing its beaux arts chaos with miles of neatly ordered, evenly spaced tower blocks. In Brasília, this ideal city seemed within the reach of architect Oscar Niemeyer (a disciple of "Corbu" who designed the buildings), and his partners, urban planner Lucio Costa (who mapped out the master plan for the new city) and Roberto Burle Marx (a landscape designer who created the federal city's numerous grand outdoor spaces). The metropolis they created looked magnificent in sketches, appears striking but slightly less wonderful in photographs and nearly sucks the life out of those doomed to live in its buildings and walk its streets.

Because Modernists believed the use of names

CLOCKWISE FROM TOP LEFT: PAULO FRIDMAN—GETTY IMAGES; BETTMANN CORBIS; JAMES DAVIS-EYE UBIQUITOUS—CORBIS

reeked of the past, everything in Brasília is designated with a number—not only the streets but also blocks, buildings and entire neighborhoods. Because in the future everyone would drive, Brasília originally had no street corners or traffic lights. These antiques were replaced by a flowing lattice of express lanes, feeder roads and traffic circles that loop through and around buildings. Because walking would soon be passé, there are no sidewalks or crossing lanes and almost none of the buildings are located within convenient walking distance of the others. Gentlemen, start your engines!

To be fair, many of the designs exhibit a breathtaking, if bloodless, beauty. Niemeyer's Alvorada Palace,

the presidential mansion, appears to float above delicate tapering columns. And all the structures impress with their big, bold shapemaking: a theater in the form of a pyramid, a cathedral that reminds some viewers of an inverted chalice or a crown of thorns lit by a resplendent stained-glass ceiling. Brasília is a collection of virtuoso objects jumbled together without any of the connective organic tissue that forges space into a community. The city's stance toward the power of government seems designed to invite awe rather than involvement. It takes a heap of livin' to make a blueprint into a home—and even at age 50, Brasília's got a heap of livin' ahead of it. ■

Reichstag

Berlin • Built: 1894; renovated: 1999
Paul Wallot, original architect
Norman Foster, architect of the renovation

After the Berlin Wall fell in 1989, the legislators of newly united Germany met in Bonn, previously the capital of West Germany. But in 1991 they decided to return the seat of government to Berlin and create a symbol of national union by restoring Germany's historic capitol building, the Reichstag. In an ironic twist of history, a British architect, Norman Foster, won the international design competition.

Created in a neoclassical style by German architect Paul Wallot and completed in 1894, the bulky, boxy old Reichstag bore the wounds of Germany's recent history. In 1933 Adolf Hitler's accomplices set fire to the building and blamed the deed on communists, assisting the Nazi leader's rise to power. Beginning in 1943 the Reichstag was bombed by Allied planes; in 1945, victorious Russian soldiers vandalized it after Hitler's fall. In a final insult, vandals of a different kind—East German designers— "restored" the building's interior on the cheap in the late 1960s and early '70s.

Wallot's building had sported a bulky cupola of steel and glass; Foster transformed it with the sort of high-tech flourish that is his trademark. The translucent dome doesn't merely squat on the building; it opens it up. The inverted, mirrored cone at its center channels light deep into the legislative chamber several stories beneath: shedding light on the work of the politicians, it acts as a brilliant metaphor for the transparency of democracy. In like manner, Foster and his team preserved some of the hundreds of graffiti messages left by Russian soldiers in 1945. But the reborn Reichstag looks to the future as well as the past: the dome of the newly green building brings solar heat into the structure, while its power plant burns clean, efficient rapeseed oil. ■

The Norman Conquest

Long the high priest of high tech, Norman Foster is now using his expertise to design a greener future for the world's cities

Novelist Ayn Rand was inspired by Frank Lloyd Wright when she created the larger-than-life character of Howard Roark, the genius form-giver of *The Fountainhead*. Were she living today, Rand might find an even better exemplar of the architect as heroic, self-made individualist in the person of Britain's Norman Foster. Seventy-six in 2010, the designer isn't content to bestride the architectural world like a colossus; rather, he hurls himself across it like a modern-day Mercury—deity of speed and commerce—as he moves among his offices in London, Hong Kong, Abu Dhabi, Madrid and New York City. He has designed London bridges, Spanish subways, Asian airports, Italian furniture. He has shaped city halls, aircraft museums, lavish yachts. Knighted by Queen Elizabeth II in 1990, Lord Foster of Thames Bank has brilliantly reinvented both the British Museum (by covering up its courtyard) and Berlin's Reichstag (by opening up its roof). Once asked to name the perfect building, he cited the Boeing 747.

Foster is no child of privilege: he was born into a working-class family in 1935 in Manchester and left school at 16 to work in the city treasurer's office, then served in the Royal Air Force. He returned to toil as a contracts manager in an architect's office and enrolled in the architecture school at the University of Manchester at age 21. His great leap forward came in the form of a fellowship for postgraduate study at Yale University; he claims he "discovered himself" in America's expansiveness, drive and promise.

At Yale, Foster roomed with fellow Briton Richard Rogers, who shared his interest in the architectural aesthetic later dubbed high tech: the use of unfinished materials and advanced technology, the inside-out exposure of infrastructure, the delight in form and movement. The two returned to England and founded the firm of Team 4 with their architect wives; their first big project was an electronics factory (since demolished), a perfect commission for their emerging industrial style. After that partnership folded, Foster's elegant design for an insurance headquarters in Ipswich made waves, and he found himself in demand.

Deep in the genetic code of the former airman's buildings is a feeling for hangar-like lightness and strength, along with frugality of consumption. A good example is his 1981 design for the airport at Stansted, England. Earlier airports had massive concentrations of ductwork above their ceilings for air conditioning, lighting and electrical services; Foster realized huge savings in structural mass and energy consumption by shifting the utilities underground, leaving a floating roof and walls that were open to natural daylight. Most major airports built since have followed suit.

When the British Museum's library moved to new premises, it left behind one of the great English spaces: the 1857 Round Reading Room, designed by Sydney Smirke, whose shallow dome was surrounded by a two-acre internal court. Foster saved the masterpiece by sweeping away the clutter of old book-stack buildings from around it and covering the court with a light-welcoming roof (2003). The ideal of humane efficiency, understood as social responsibility, undergirds much of Foster's work: he is frequently cited as one of the great visionaries of green design. In Frankfurt's highly influential Commerzbank Tower (1997), he built a supertower that blooms with garden atriums and uses natural ventilation (vs. fuel-gobbling air conditioning) for 60% of the year. Innovative "sunscoops" funnel natural light into many of his buildings. "Foster doesn't merely prove that great architects can be great designers," TIME critic Richard Lacayo wrote in 2007. "He proves that they can be good citizens too." ∎

REICHSTAG BUILDING DOME, BERLIN, 1999

Foster's spiral ramp resembles the interior of Frank Lloyd Wright's Guggenheim Museum in New York City. The transparent dome offers views across united Berlin, while the cone of mirrored glass at its center diffuses and reflects natural light deep into the historic building's cavernous interior, illuminating the workings of the legislators.

MILLENNIUM BRIDGE, LONDON, 2000

When the bridge was opened, enormous crowds flocked to cross it—and the roadway began wobbling. It was closed and additional structural support was added, while British tabloids jeered, dubbing Foster "Lord Wobbly." Foster is helping remake modern London: he will remodel Trafalgar Square and his 2004 Gherkin Building is the toast of the City of London.

"High tech is misleading … You can't separate technology from the humanistic, spiritual content of a building." —NORMAN FOSTER

BRITISH MUSEUM COURTYARD, LONDON, 2003
Foster saved the museum library's vintage Reading Room and created a vast entrance area by stripping away a jumble of storage buildings that encircled the structure and covering the courtyard with a steel-and-glass roof that filled the space with light. Some call Foster's work sterile; British writer Will Self said of this space: "Never has a finished building looked so much like its computer visualization."

COMMERZBANK TOWER, FRANKFURT, GERMANY, 1997
A milestone in environmental design, the building was the world's greenest skyscraper when completed. Nine three-story gardens bloom at various levels of the 850-ft. (259 m) tower, which has a 12-story garden atrium at its heart. Office windows open to let in natural air, and toilets flush with "gray water" from cooling towers. Water-filled grids in ceilings cool offices in summer, while solar power helps heat them in winter.

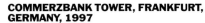

CHEK LAP KOK AIRPORT, HONG KONG, 1998
The world's largest airport—Foster calls it a "horizontal cathedral"—was built on an artificial island. Inside, the architect enclosed 125 acres under one roof to create the world's largest single room, the size of more than 100 football fields. Foster helped reimagine the modern airport by reversing the placement of infrastructure, opening the buildings to light and air.

Buildings That Surprise

Stiltsville, Biscayne Bay, Florida
Originally created as fishing shacks, some of these fanciful structures outside Miami were later developed into homes and social clubs. There were 27 such buildings in 1960; only seven remain

Buildings of Glass
The architecture of transparency

When Joseph Paxton's revolutionary Crystal Palace opened as the home of London's Great Exhibition of 1851, it created an uproar. Critics denounced it as little more than an overgrown greenhouse; some even compared it to plumbing. But the new building won far more admirers than detractors: dappled with light and shadow, uplifting visitors with its vast vaulted concourse, this showplace of glass was an inspiring, ennobling space. And it was more: this was the first great building of the Industrial Age, a structure that pointed the way toward the future, as it demonstrated that the era's new materials—plate glass and iron—could create exciting new shapes that captured the energy of the times in physical form.

The building was assembled from prefabricated units and erected in only three months by semi-skilled workers. Although it was designed to be disassembled after the two-year exhibition, it was so beloved that it was moved to a park in south London, where it stood for many years before it was destroyed by fire in 1936. (The building's portability was further proof of its technological novelty.) With its curtain walls of metal and glass, the building is the direct predecessor of the modern skyscraper and of other breathtaking buildings of glass, from train depots to homes to chapels. ■

CRYSTAL PALACE, LONDON, 1851
British architect Joseph Paxton was a former gardener who learned the secrets of iron-and-glass construction in building palm courts and lily houses. The walls and roof of this famed building were constructed from 293,000 sheets of plate glass.

THORNCROWN CHAPEL, ARKANSAS, 1980
Architect E. Fay Jones, a disciple of Frank Lloyd Wright's, designed this graceful chapel to blend into the forested bluffs of the Ozark Mountains outside Eureka Springs in northern Arkansas. The walls of the 48-ft. (15 m) -high building are covered by more than 6,000 sq. ft. of glass.

WINTER GARDEN, NEW YORK CITY, 1988
A glass vault in the shape of a tapering cornucopia covers the centerpiece of a retail gallery and pedestrian arcade at the World Financial Center in Battery Park City in Manhattan. Severely damaged in the 9/11 terrorist attacks, it reopened on Sept. 17, 2002.

GLASS HOUSE, CONNECTICUT, 1949
American architect Philip Johnson, a disciple of Ludwig Mies van der Rohe's and a leading figure of both Modernist and post-Modernist design, built this see-through retreat in New Canaan in 1949, using an open-plan interior in the style of Mies.

IGLOO, CANADIAN ARCTIC

The Inuit igloo above costs nothing, aside from labor, to construct. Made of snow packed into cubes, it is reinforced on the inside as the heat of a fire melts the inner walls to form a solid shield of ice, sealing any chinks in the walls and helping retain interior heat. This building "moves" in a special way, disappearing as the ice blocks melt and turn into water.

Buildings That Move
The architecture of impermanence

Designers wrestle with blueprints to achieve a wide variety of goals: loftiness, size, comfort, thrift, majesty, efficiency. But portability is seldom among them. One exception, Joseph Paxton's great Crystal Palace in London, was a prefabricated structure that was assembled in only three months in 1851, then taken down and rebuilt elsewhere. Moshe Safdie's famed Habitat, a stack-of-cubes 1970s apartment complex in Montreal, was not mobile, but its modular design was intended to launch a new era of more mobile construction, in which precast concrete units could be easily moved and assembled on-site to provide inexpensive housing in growing cities. But Habitat did not lead to the revolution Safdie hoped for.

To find buildings that are truly portable, we must turn to the world's nomads, whose domiciles are a form of folk technology developed over countless generations. The structural apparatus of such buildings is generally taken from the tent: an infrastructure of wooden poles or lathes is covered by skins or canvas to create a dry shelter from rain and wind.

The sublime exception to this rule is the igloo of ice constructed by the Inuit people of the Arctic regions, which achieves a kind of perfection in both its shape and its materials. Like all domes, it is the most efficient way to cover space and provide shelter, and its essential materials, snow and ice, are abundantly available, for free. It is one of mankind's most practical buildings. ■

GER, MONGOLIA

Nomadic Mongols erect several different types of portable homes, or yurts. The most elaborate and widely used of them is the ger, right, which features a lower circular rim or wall with a wood lattice that elevates the ceiling inside. Most gers have post-and-lintel doorways, limiting their portability.

NATIVE AMERICAN TEEPEE, DAKOTA TERRITORY, 1880

The classic American teepee, below right, maximizes floor space by combining a pyramid shape with a tent-style support system whose masts are tree branches stripped and lashed together. Simpler than the ger, the teepee is thus more portable.

CHAMBAREH, IRAN

The Shâhsavan (also known as Ilsovan) nomads of Iran's plains erect dome-shaped yurts, or chambareh, below, that can be taken down and put up in less than an hour. Beneath the hide covering is a skeleton of bow-shaped sticks that converge at the top center and slot into a circular ring. The chambareh lacks the lower wooden rim that shapes the walls of the Mongolian ger.

Suspended Buildings
The architecture of tension

Easy to assemble, efficient in function and based on materials that are widely available in nature, the tent is one of mankind's oldest, humblest structures. Most tents, like the Native American teepee or Mongolian ger, are composed of an exterior of cloth or hide that covers an interior framework. But when 20th century architects set out to reinvent the tent with modern materials, they turned to a more sophisticated form, in which the roof of the structure is held up by wires attached to tall supporting masts. The engineering is similar to that of a suspension bridge.

The suspension format is an efficient way to shelter a large area, and its most interesting applications have come at large sporting venues. One of the first such structures was the Yoyogi National Sports Center in Tokyo, the primary setting for the 1964 Olympic Games. Japanese architect Kenzo Tange hung the roof of the large arena from two tall supporting masts, eliminating the need for supporting columns, thus ensuring unobscured sight lines from each of its 15,000 seats.

German architect Otto Frei demonstrated the unique capabilities of suspension memorably at the 1972 Munich Games. Frei suspended multiple roofs over sections of the Olympic complex, including the main arena, still in use. The covering offers spectators basic shelter from sun and rain, but it is distinguished by its beauty as well as its utility. Made of PVC-coated polyester fabric, the roof is light in feeling and alive with circulating breezes, while it is also beautifully luminous, a dappled scrim between spectator and sky through which clouds can be seen. Small wonder contemporary architects' interest in tents is intense. ∎

MUNICH OLYMPIC STADIUM, 1972
Though seating completely surrounds the elliptical main stadium at top center, its translucent roof covers only the seats most exposed to the glare of direct sunlight. Tents also shade the pedestrian arcades at bottom.

RINGLING BROS. CIRCUS TENT, U.S., 1956

The tent has long been associated with the itinerant circus form of entertainment. The legendary Big Top used by the Ringling Bros. and Barnum & Bailey Circus was large enough to shelter three performance rings and 16,000 spectators. Elephants were harnessed to help hoist the four main supporting masts at the building's center into position. Above, the last time the Ringling Bros. Circus performed under its big canopy was at an appearance outside Pittsburgh, Pa., in 1956.

YOYOGI NATIONAL SPORTS CENTER, TOKYO, 1964

Suspending his twin roofs from masts, Kenzo Tange created swooping, organic forms that are demonstrations of tensile strength in action. (Only the top portion of the second roof, on left, can be seen here.) Like the roofs, the central support structure descends in the middle between the two main masts at either end of the building. A central skylight allows natural light into the arena.

Offbeat Buildings
Architecture out of bounds

We can't tell you what the home of the future will look like, but we're prepared to wager it probably won't bear any resemblance to the sci-fi saucer at far right, which was designed by Finnish architect Matti Suuronen and marketed in the 1960s in two versions, Futuro I and Futuro II. Made of reinforced plastic and originally envisioned to be used as ski cabins, the *Jetsons*-style homes were manufactured and sold in kit form through such sources as *The Whole Earth Catalog*.

The Futuro's nifty circular floor plan includes a central fireplace (with space for a stereo conveniently located beneath the hearth) and streamlined seats that convert into beds. And when it's time to come down to earth: "Deploy the retractable stairs!" They are adjustable, permitting the home to remain level on sloping terrain. About 20 of the houses are still believed to be in use around the world.

Perhaps even more unusual than the Futuro house is a hotel made of ice. But when the Hotel Glace (Ice Hotel), modeled after a Swedish original, opened its doors outside Quebec City in the winter of 2000, it was an immediate hit. The hotel features walls of snow that are 4 ft. (1.2 m) thick; interior temperatures are between 23° and 28°F. One of the most frequently asked questions on the Ice Hotel website: What about rest rooms? Potential visitors are advised that a heated facility awaits their use.

And though it perhaps belongs in the story on houses that move, we've included here a brilliant exercise in streamlining, the Airstream Clipper mobile home, the brainchild of onetime advertising copywriter Wally Byam, which first went on sale in 1936. Devotees still haul the trusty trailers across the U.S. and gather annually to form "silver cities." ∎

TREEHOUSE RESORT, OREGON
The Out 'n' About "treesort" is one of a number of bed-and-breakfasts worldwide that offer cabins in the trees. Visitors to the Oregon retreat choose from 18 cabins, from 8 to 52 ft. (2.5 to 16 m) aboveground. Kids play on swinging bridges, rope ladders and a ropes course.

AIRSTREAM TRAILERS
Wally Byam, Airstream's founder, was a visionary who incorporated aircraft design—a riveted aluminum exterior and streamlined styling—into his travel trailer. The original 1936 Clipper sold for $1,200. Enthusiasts continue to converge at remote sites to swap tales of life on the road—and to swap imaginative Airstream accessories.

FUTURO II, 1968
The prefabricated home designed by Finn Matti Suuronen was made of reinforced plastic; it sold with a complete interior for $14,000. When a global oil crisis struck in the early 1970s, plastic prices soared, making production costs prohibitive.

ICE HOTEL, QUEBEC CITY
Everything in the hotel—columns, floors, ceilings, beds, tables, barstools and the registration counter—is made of ice. The structure changes each year; in 2004, shown at left, there were 31 rooms and 10 suites. Two art galleries and a movie theater were on the premises, and in case things heated up, the facility included an all-ice wedding chapel.

TAIL O' THE PUP, LOS ANGELES, 1945

Scholars call buildings whose form deliberately apes their function examples of "programmatic" or "representational" architecture, but we call it WYSIWYG: what you see is what you get. The breed is a favorite with retail establishments looking to be noticed. A beloved Los Angeles hot-dog stand, Tail o' the Pup was almost torn down in the 1980s but was moved to a new location and survived until 2006, when the property owner chose not to renew its lease.